Chasing the Sky

20 Stories of Women in Architecture

Contents:

Introduction 6
Foreword 8
Emma Williamson 12
Camilla Block 26
Hannah Tribe 38
Rachel Nolan 52
Stephanie Little 66
Tara Veldman 82
Penny Fuller 94
Sarah Ball 108
Debbie Ryan 120
Rachel Neeson 134

Sue Carr 150
Melissa Bright 164
Lisa-Maree Carrigan 174
Clare Cousins 186
Abbie Galvin 200
Ingrid Richards 214
Annabel Lahz 226
Christina Na-Heon Cho 238
Kerstin Thompson 248
Virginia Kerridge 262
Colophon 278

Introduction

Dean Dewhirst

It is my great pleasure to introduce to you *Chasing the Sky*, a book that showcases twenty of Australia's leading women in architecture. *Chasing the Sky* is the second book in the '20 Stories' series, with each edition featuring different aspects of the architecture industry.

Maven

In my role structuring senior teams, I have noticed a rise in the call for more women in leadership and have seen the benefits of this development. Diversification in leadership fosters a healthy workplace culture but behind the scenes I am witnessing the rising talent—our emerging leaders—eschewing male-dominated practices in favour of those with gender equality. Those organisations that are embracing women are reaping the benefits. They are progressive practices seen as creative and future-forward.

It is my hope that you will see these women, their stories and their achievements for what they are and enjoy getting to know them, just as I have. It's impossible to read the captivating tales and witness the extraordinary portfolios assembled in this collection without recognising these individuals as the highly talented and industry mavens they are.

These stories capture the buzz of architecture: the smell of building sites, the precision of lines and of creating something tangible from something ethereal. They also capture the strength of character required to rise to the top in Australian architecture, to take opportunities for what they are, no matter how small or irrelevant they may seem at the time, to be flexible and lateral thinking, and to allow oneself to be mentored.

Most of all what I drew from this diverse cross-section of women in Australian architecture is the sense of community and support for each other, the industry and the young people coming through. And that was the most encouraging sign: to know that there is both a legacy and a pathway for those that follow, which can only lead to a stronger and more creative architecture industry for the future.

Foreword

Maryam Gusheh

Growing up in 1970s Tehran, I have fond memories of site inspections with my mother, a structural engineer on large-scale civic developments. I recall her in high-heeled, firm-fitting brown leather boots as she marched across fields of concrete and steel, elegantly poised, confident. On reflection, tall working boots were the order of the day in post-war Iran, where an accelerated programme of state-led modernisation sponsored higher education for women.

Economic growth, fast-paced urbanisation and demand for expert knowledge had secured the contribution of female professionals at an unprecedented scale; so much so that for my sister and I, our friends and contemporaries, a vibrant working life was not only probable or desired, but appeared inevitable.

In *Chasing the Sky* the concentrated voice of some of Australia's most dynamic practitioners, and their substantial projects, compel us to strive for just such possibility; for equitable and vital architectural careers in our immediate reach. Distilled in this volume is a palpable sense of women at work in architecture, of the joys and challenges of a creative profession and the culture of making.

Common themes and questions run across the volume to reveal commonalities and differences. We hear varied views on education, craft and technology; on collaboration and inventive processes; on formative influences and entrepreneurship; and, on the relationship between architecture and society. We see these priorities as instilled in the city fabric, in homes and public works and everyday urban settings.

One of the most engaging aspects of the book is the rich sense of the architectural community. As acclaimed individuals and as a diverse collective, they offer an incisive glimpse into the richness of contemporary Australian architecture, of the spirit that galvanises the profession and cultivates its future buoyancy.

UNSW
Australia

Chasing the Sky

20 Stories of Women in Architecture

Emma Williamson

Design generosity

Emma is a founding director of CODA Studio. A practice she started with her husband Kieran straight out of university twenty years ago. The practice has grown from humble beginnings to complete award-winning projects across all scales from urban design and master planning to architecture and interiors.

1 / 20

Emma studied architecture and interior design at Curtin University and went on to teach in both disciplines over a ten-year period combining this with practice.
In 2006 she decided to practice full time, focusing her attention on the growth and culture of the studio as well as a particular interest in interiors. In addition to practice she is on the AIA National Committee for Gender Equity, is a Senior Adjunct Research Fellow at Monash University and is regularly asked to participate on national juries for awards and competitions. As CODA, Emma and Kieran have a combined vision to create buildings and places that have a backbone of social integrity and give generously to the community.

A backbone of social justice and the idea of being useful have been big drivers in the work we have pursued and produce in our practice.

Bunbury Catholic College
In a joint venture with Broderick Architects, CODA was commissioned to undertake master planning and design of this new campus. The completed stage one buildings form the formal civic heart of the campus, with the following stages to be constructed over the next decade.

Concrete perfume

It is one thing to be drawn to something and another to have your interest sustained. There are so many dimensions to architecture and it is such a fantastically complex and broad discipline. No matter where you are there is rich fuel for thought if you look backwards or forwards. In our own practice this comes from our collaborations within the studio and with others and the complexity that comes from understanding what a client needs.

I come from a huge 'combined' family. None of my parents were architects, or even in building, they have always had lots of architect friends and value creativity. I have always been a great maker of things and the idea of creating spaces and working with materials in a rigorous and inventive way is appealing. I like the idea of starting with a series of constraints and finding the best possible solution to the specifics of that challenge. Responding to a set of conditions or a problem is still a real driver for me and one of the reasons that I enjoy working on interiors projects so much.

In the early years of my 'Brady Bunch' family arrangement there were too many children in too few bedrooms. Eventually the decision was made to buy a new house that could accommodate us all. An enormous derelict Federation house was found in the suburb where we lived. Brian Klopper was hired as the architect tasked to add another five bedrooms, a living and dining room. I was only about nine at the time and this very tall man with work boots and a big roll of drawings made a big

Photography — Peter Bennetts

impression on me. I absolutely loved seeing the original house come back to life and the incredible extension grafted on to the back.

My mother is an artist and my upbringing was full of conversation about art, furniture, and food. They were all considered important creative aspects of our life and lots of this rubbed off on me.

My parents were also socially active and there was always a great cause being fought from our living room! This could range from work for the Nuclear Disarmament Party, to the Medical Association for the Prevention of War to trying to ban war toys. This backbone of social justice and the idea of being useful has been a big driver in the work we have pursued in our practice.

I started studying architecture at Curtin University straight out of school in the late 1980s. During my studies I took two big breaks and moved to Sydney both times to work in practices. The first time I worked in a large commercial practice in North Sydney. It really wasn't my thing. The work was very dry, there seemed to be almost no interaction with the client and the client was rarely the user. I just wasn't convinced the designs were really improving things for people.

The second time I decided I'd be very specific and targeted a job in only two very small practices. Luckily I managed to get one (with Durbach Block Jaggers) and I worked there for eighteen months. That was a completely different thing all together. Super long hours, intense scrutiny of the design and process, as well as lots of interaction with clients. This really changed my view about what was possible and what I wanted.

In my final two years of university I started going out with my now husband Kieran. We both had strong ideas about what we wanted from architecture and what we thought we could do. Having this partnership helped me to take some risks early on.

Starting in practice

When Kieran and I finished university there was a lack of opportunity in Perth to work for an interesting practice. I became an academic and we combined this with establishing our own practice.

The combination of these two things, and the regular income from teaching, meant we were able to work toward the type of practice we really wanted to create. Being a business owner is challenging in so many ways. Having staff means you need to be on the look out for them as well. There have been moments when we have been overwhelmed with personal situations completely outside of our control that impact on the studio in the biggest possible way. These are probably the most difficult because there is a limit to how much you can do. I've come to accept that it's just not always possible to have clarity with so many lives in the mix.

I think growing a business while you are growing your family is difficult work and is often overlooked! If I look back to when our kids were babies the memories are hazy. I'm not sure if I've blocked them out and moved on or I can't remember because I was so sleep deprived! Even now, with older children, there are weeks where the juggle makes me feel like a character in some kind of comedy; as I try to race about putting out fires and catching spinning plates with one hand behind my back and with a blindfold on.

Beautiful reward

Architecture has enabled me to imagine a future through the interlinking of optimism and freedom. It has made me curious, made me ask questions, and helped me to develop a collaborative approach to problem solving.

Photography – Peter Bennetts

Throughout history land ownership and development has been a battleground. I think the current development process challenges the necessity of architects, but not the credibility of architects.

It's liberating not to be looking for one answer and it's exciting to be curious and optimistic about the future. I feel like this is a freedom that I have every day, that I take to every situation no matter what it is. I am free to consider and reimagine anything I please.

It's hard to not sound cliché but the biggest joy I get is working with clients that enjoy the process; who trust we will listen to them; trust that we will come up with a good solution and then love the outcome. I really love getting to know the client and listening to people's stories. There is incredible richness in this and an opportunity to tease these out and reveal a way forward for a project that reflects their aspirations and its history.

I am always very conscious of the fact that a building will last longer than I will. Once the project is over the building needs to have a full and happy life with its users. For that to happen the building needs to reflect the client's aspirations not just an idea imposed by an architect.

The greatest joy is imagining something and getting everyone to collaborate in realising this. We have such a great studio of people working collaboratively toward this common goal.

As my career has progressed, I have become increasingly amazed that buildings ever get to site—it's almost against the odds! The complexity of briefing, approvals, finance and changing circumstances means there is always, in my mind, a chance the project will only ever be an idea. So when a project does get to site it involves a complex mix of emotions. I exhale and then inevitably have a moment when I doubt everything. It's a big responsibility designing buildings—we use so many resources, spend so much money and involve so many people in the process—I just cannot take it lightly. Once I get this out of my system and reconnect with the project I feel really excited for everyone. It really is incredible to make something so complex.

Progressing the profession

Throughout history land ownership and development has been a battleground. I think the current development process challenges the necessity of architects, but not the credibility of architects. As our representative body the Australian Institute of Architects needs to advocate for the relevance of architects in matters of the city and ensure we get a seat at the table.

For some reason, as architects we have separated ourselves from the politics of the city. We have been slow to react to the erosion of our jobs, as more and more specialists have established themselves as expert in everything from urban design to placemaking, project management to brief writing. This means more people come between us and a direct relationship with the client.

The development process is changing and architects need to operate from a position of strength. We need to be agile. We need to work out how to solve big problems while speaking the language that has currency for all of the players in the development process.

Certainly the young architects that we connect with through our studio are committed to the idea of progressing humanity through architecture. Working for the benefit of many rather than a few was a big driver for us to grow CODA away from a single residential client base. There are competing forces in construction and it is not always easy to contribute to social change in the way we might have hoped to in the early days. I look at businesses like the mobile laundry service for the homeless and think that really does something immediate, necessary and useful. It does it quickly and can help many. Architecture is by nature a slow moving beast. I think it's hard to feel like you are making big changes in the way that you might like in the face of such lags in time.

Over time we have shifted to working 'invisibly' on projects where we feel we can make a change for the better. This is a shift away from the object and into a space where we help when there are roadblocks. Sometimes this has been for community groups through pro-bono work. Other times it is for large government bodies advising, as architects, on the best approach to subdivision and development of land. Sometimes a building is not the answer to a problem but this does not mean that it is not the job of an architect to come up with an answer.

Gender parity

There is a long way to go before we have anything that even closely resembles gender equity in architecture. Awards that celebrate women and shine a light on their achievements specifically are important to changing attitudes over time. We will know that we have achieved equity when we don't need these any more.

I think it is also important to consider the gender bias that exists for men as well as women. Perhaps if men felt more able to create a flexible work arrangement for themselves without it resulting in a career disadvantage they would be in a better position to contribute more equally to the dynamics of family life.

Rising above commonplace

I am inspired by people who rethink things that we take for granted. Those who show agility and generosity no matter what they are doing. I am very fortunate to be surrounded by lots of inspirational people!

I am inspired by people who rethink things that we take for granted. Those who show agility and generosity no matter what they are doing.

Photography — Peter Bennetts

As I approach architecture from the point of problem solving I need to be open, absorb all types of influences and think laterally about how to make connections between things.

Our practice life is not just concerned with making buildings. It is also concerned with making a difference for everyone that interacts with it.

My life can, at times, get quite chaotic. Balancing the demands of studio and family isn't always easy and we also make a big effort to engage with our community. Doing this gives us a chance to connect with a cross-section of amazing people who are similarly driven to be useful. This can range from engaging with our school community, sitting on the AIA Gender Equity Committee, the philanthropic pursuits of Impact 100, pro-bono work or pursuing a project with the Green Party. Through all of this we are constantly reminded of the inspiring focus and diversity of people that make for such a rich life.

— *Do you think the present education system measures up?* Interestingly I think the classical model of architectural education is very, very relevant. It may even make its way into mainstream education in the future. Contemporary education suggests that the future should be more collaborative, more project based and involve more problem solving. All of these things are firmly imbedded in architectural education. If I had a criticism about the education system it would be around the demands that the institutions have had to place on feedback and assessment. The cycle of accountability has reduced the appetite for risk and as a result there is a real potential to accept the mediocre as the norm.

Claisebrook Design Community
An existing sawtooth roof warehouse and double storey office was transformed to create a connected and dynamic business development hub. The rear warehouse provides room for an open event space, workshop and individual working pods. The internal cafe also provides an important connection to the surrounding community.

I think true innovation is produced through risk and failure—and the willingness to learn from this.

— *What advice would you give a student when they hit a brick wall?* I don't think there is such a thing as an insurmountable brick wall. My advice would be to don't try to solve the problem on your own. Architecture is collaborative, so have a conversation with someone. Create a diagram or timeline on the way you will approach the smaller problems as a way of getting over the wall.

— *What qualities do you look for when hiring for your practice?* Cultural fit is a key driver for us. We have been fortunate to have exceptional people apply to work here. Being explicit about our values and what drives us means they know what they are signing up for. Curiosity, agility, humour, honesty, generosity [these are all qualities we would rate highly] and a love of good food. It might sound weird but we have found in the past that this is a really good indicator of someone fitting in to our studio. We eat together once a week and take it in turns to prepare lunch. Sharing food is a big part of how we connect.

Radical transformation

There have been massive shifts in architecture since I started with a drawing board! At the same time as a project team is now made up of millions of specialists we seem to have more and more liability

Photography — Peter Bennetts

Life Lessons

1

Emma Williamson

- Taking risks early on is easier when you have fewer responsibilities
- Agile thinking within constraints can deliver unexpected outcomes
- Use your skills to make a social contribution beyond buildings
- Listen to people's stories to really understand what is important and what is needed
- Reconnect with the policies of your city and look for opportunities
- Equity in practice is about men and women
- Show generosity in everything you do
- Successful architects need to be good communicators
- True innovation is produced through risk and failure

Photography — Peter Bennetts

I really believe that the discipline of learning to draw by hand helps us to develop critical thinking. In the absence of the delete button we are much more likely to consider ideas before we put pen to paper.

Photography — Peter Bennetts

for the work we do. The internet allows us to share work in a way that has connected places like Western Australia, where we practice. So projects are happening in real time and become a part of a current debate about what's happening. When I started out I would have to wait to see projects in magazines and international ones in books. Now I see them daily thanks to Instagram.

My concern with computerisation is that one can so easily get lost in making minute decisions at completely the wrong time without developing a strong overall position on a project. A strong idea should be scalable but the computer offers no scale. So my nervousness is based on the way we approach the computer as it doesn't offer a solution, it is just a tool. We need to think first and then act! I really believe that the discipline of learning to draw by hand helps us to develop critical thinking. In the absence of the delete button we are much more likely to consider ideas before we put pen to paper.

Photography — Peter Bennetts

Karratha Super Clinic
The design responds to the cultural values of indigenous clients; particularly how they experience enclosed spaces and the understanding of cultural traditions for privacy.

Camilla Block

The dreamers are on the roof

Camilla Block graduated from the University of Sydney with a Bachelor of Architecture (First Class Honours) in 1991 and joined Neil Durbach in practice in 1992. In 1998, the office of Durbach Block Architects was established.

2 / 20

Camilla worked as the project director on the Droga Apartment, which received the National RAIA Robin Boyd Award for Housing and the RAIA Wilkinson Award for Housing (NSW). Camilla has been a design principal involved in all of the major projects of Durbach Block, which includes the University of Technology Sydney (UTS) Thomas Street Science Building, Roslyn Street Kings Cross, the Brickpit Ring, Holman House, House Spry, Commonwealth Place, Canberra, and Sydney Amenities Buildings Homebush Bay. She has also, lectured, exhibited, judged awards and been published both nationally and internationally.
In 2014, Camilla received an honorary appointment as Adjunct Professor from UTS, Faculty Design Architecture and Building. Camilla's unique perspectives on 'thinking and seeing' puts architecture in a very happy place indeed.

I gave my nine year old daughter a book for Christmas called 'Miss Happiness and Miss Flower' by Rumer Godden. I presented it to her saying, "This is why I became an architect." She is still at an age where she half hopes she could be a demigod daughter of Athena or a mermaid. So a book that turns you into an architect has slightly less appeal.

5-9 Roslyn Street, Potts Point
A four-storey commercial building overcomes the challenges of a triangular shaped site less than 200m2 in size. The cornice is exaggerated to overhang the street, to suggest a room. On the street, it appears to be an ephemeral version of the neighbourhood buildings. An exotic roof top garden of Frangipani trees and seasonal plantings is framed in the sky through buckled openings. At the corner the building shifts to being strongly surfaced, curving in two directions, to create a peninsular of moulded light.

Photography — Julia Charles

From the ground up

The book tells the story of Nona, an immigrant child, building a Japanese house for two dolls called Miss Happiness and Miss Flower. The slow and careful description of how the house and garden are lovingly conceived by Nona, and built by her older cousin Tom, was unwittingly my introduction to the beauty of research, design and coercion. A gift of a seven-centimetre willow bonsai tree magically completes the garden—a perfect world in miniature. At the end of the book, after so many words, there are drawings of the house, plans, details, even an exploded axonometric. It was as if the whole book led to this, a short cut, pictures not words. It was a revelation for me. The house was no longer a story—it could be real.

In a way, I was much like Nona. Immigrating young to Australia from South Africa, I have found a way to make and remake a home, understanding a new place through architecture. After a landscape lost, architecture became a way back in, a way to see, to interpret and to belong. South Africa is a wild and unregulated place today. It was even more so when I was little. My mother, who is prone to making her own rules anyway, believed that building sites were common territory. In her view, theses sites did not belong to anyone until the moving trucks had pulled away from the curb.

Photographs — Neil Durbach

My childhood was unaccompanied by TV—imagine that! One of the things we used to do to entertain ourselves was to take walks around our neighborhood and investigate half completed buildings. These were not great works of architecture. Mostly houses and gardens under construction, piles of sand, foundation lines, and big holes. But I remember trying to puzzle it out. What was it going to be? Completing, wondering, adjusting, finishing the beginning. It felt natural to me. This kind of 'thinking-seeing' was another beginning for me. I was nine when I first came to Australia on a visit. One of the most compelling memories of this visit for me was seeing the Sydney Opera House for the first time. I remember it as more like a very still beast, a giant open structure that we were free to touch, climb on, and not even quietly. It was profoundly and immediately mine in a tactile and intuitive way.

Learning a new language

The magic of looking at and visiting great buildings began in earnest for me at Sydney University. Sue Rice and Richard Leplastrier taught us to read the language of buildings. To understand their ideas, stories, hierarchies and guiding structures. My then, Fifth Year design tutor, Neil Durbach, would say, "What would Le Corbusier/Kahn/Siza do?". In pre-internet days, Neil was his own search engine. He would send one of us to the library saying something like "go and fetch a back issue of Architectural Design from late 1984 on the Stirling project for the Braun Factory." While the student was gone, he would begin to describe the project, drawing its essential components, in plan and in section, weaving a story in words at the same time. It was so suggestive, so magically evocative, when the real project finally turned up, it was sometimes a disappointment. Designing buildings at university began with learning this almost hidden language and then trying to articulate and emulate it through designing and representing our own projects. Understanding architectural diagrams is not simple but very beautiful. It is not academic or historical. It is not a timeline of style or elements. It is a diagram of parts in plan and in section; an abstract narrative or distillation of the arrangement of parts or movement, or all of these. A clarity and depth of thinking that can be read into a great building of an age. This is 'thinking-seeing-drawing'—a shorthand that abstracts and annotates analysis to aid understanding and memory. In this way, we were taught how others think and made architecture. To be humble and think ourselves into other minds—to really see—suspend disbelief and learn many ways.

David Malouf talks about being a writer and slipping into other skins, saying 'a person who is in two minds about everything, and when he's given it a bit of thought finds that he's in six minds about it.'

Doing and dreaming

Neil Durbach and I have worked together for 25 years now. We share a South African background and a sense of humour. We share a construction sensibility, a preference for sculptural form and solidity to a detailed expression of parts.

Same fabric
makes a
streetscape,
and a
sculptural
end

Life Lessons

2

Camilla Block

- Architecture is always a beginning, always curious
- Travel for architects is an essential refresh
- If you can't draw you are unarmed
- Understanding architectural diagrams is not simple but very beautiful
- Learn early on to read the hidden language of buildings
- Don't attempt everything, just try to achieve something with conviction and focus
- Demolition is a cautionary tale to try and build something worth keeping
- You need to love it to survive it
- Having a sense of humour in challenging times is sometimes the last barrier to insanity

Brickpit Ring
The Brickpit is a place of extraordinary human endeavour. It is a portrait of land disturbance through use. An aerial walkway and outdoor exhibition, twenty metres above the brick pit floor, the Ring Walk gives the brick pit a genuine urban connection and presence within Sydney Olympic Park. Interlaced with interpretive devices, the ring provides visitors with perspectives into the history of the brick pit and its use as a wildlife refuge.
Photography — Craig Karlstrom

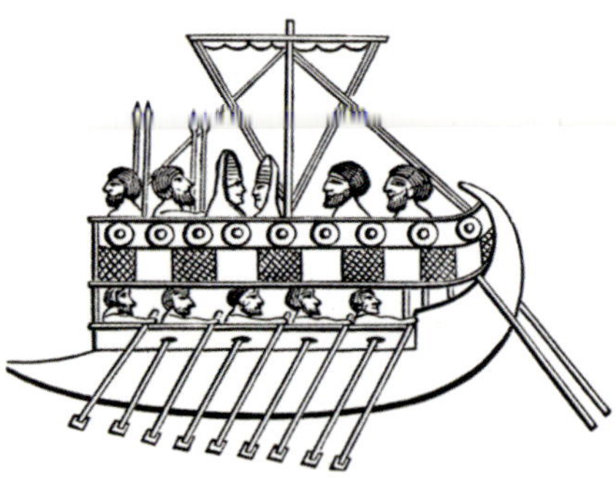

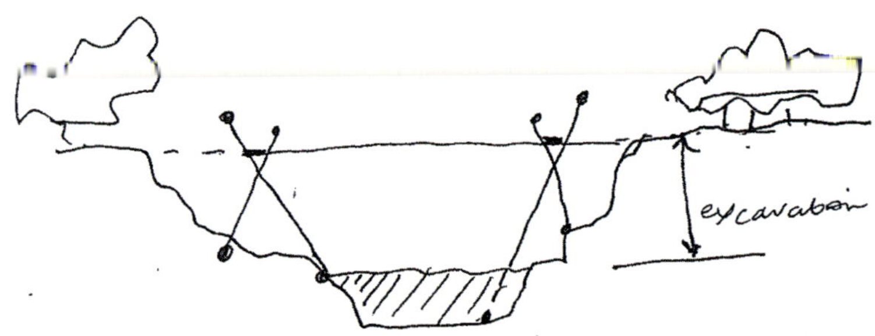

We have built a practice, together with David Jaggers, the third leg of the tripod and in many ways the stabiliser. We are lucky to work in our own building—a large studio in Potts Point that we share with Neeson Murcutt, Joseph Grech and Sue Barnsley, with a beautiful roof top garden and meeting space above. I like the idea of this drawing [above]. There is a galley of grinders doing the hard yards below and the dreamers are on the roof. In fact in a small office like ours, we are rushing up and down the stairs all day doing both jobs—doing and dreaming. In the hurly burly of small practice, there is an enormous pleasure and stability in long collaboration. There is the shorthand of a common history, shared mistakes and successes. Also enough trust to take risks, and enough respect to rely on borrowed filters of each other's perspectives. I am always astonished by the chemistry of a design conversation; the alchemy that combines distinct and separate thoughts into something unforeseen, unexpected, and sometimes right.

— *What qualities do you look for when hiring for your practice?* We are a small practice with limited seats so we choose carefully. Essentials are a love of architecture, integrity, broad skills, can-do spirit, open ended thinking, and un-preciousness when it comes to role descriptions. The ability to see the big picture and maintaining a sense of humour in challenging times is sometimes the last barrier to insanity.

Beautiful reward

Architecture is always a beginning, always curious—it is endlessly challenging. It has been a forgiving receptacle for all my changing loves, interests and thoughts. Our practice is underpinned by the tenets of open curiosity and work loved into existence by intense working and reworking. It is never simple, always demanding of the better self, the next idea. I like to think we keep our borders loose, we drift between languages, eclectically mixing current loves with old obsessions, lifting and shifting cues from contexts, absorbing and transforming, aiming for clarity of purpose and joyfulness of form. I love being on site, watching the picture slowly come into focus. It's a bit like gardening but faster and someone else is getting dirty. I do have a secret love of demolition too, maybe because it is so quick. All the things you thought were so solid, so permanent, gone in what feels like an instant. Then months of slow crawl to recreate. Demolition in itself is a cautionary tale to try and build something worth keeping.

— *Has there been a moment when you felt as if the roof fell in?* Architects walk a tightrope between trying to anticipate as much as we can, knowing that it is not possible to have a complete documentation set, and then delegating the delivery to others, the builder and subcontractors. Every time a drawing is slightly wrong, I still die a little. However, I have now learned to panic inwardly and focus on solving the problem. There is a huge difference between the neat

If you can't draw you are unarmed. This is how you contribute in real time to the messy, iterative, in-the-now process that is called design. Drawing is the only thing builders think they can't do better than you.

office world of paper and five millimetre tolerances and the messy scale of site—dirt, water, blokes, trucks, and weather. There have been some scary moments: the specification for a small urinal in a restaurant turned out to be the kindergarten sized 'boy' model. Moody lighting, slightly inebriated patrons and a urinal the size of a teacup... not good. The scariest of all, when the piling rig toppled at the Holman House site, saved only by a small wall from crashing seventy meters into the sea.

Rising above commonplace

— *Does today's education system really measure up?* Teaching architecture has always been a fractured business it seems—a bit of this and that, playing catch-up with the current concerns. But architectural design is always our cultural heart, to make good buildings whose quality and contribution might ensure their longevity. Students somehow learn this, through mentoring and inspiration, despite the varied course load. This is our skill and should always be the baseline of architectural education.

— *What advice would you give a student when they hit a wall?* There is huge difference between coverage and depth. Don't attempt everything—just try something with conviction and focus. Sometimes just doing an ordinary building well is hard enough. Look at the work of others to remind you what is possible. Don't hide behind words. Look at buildings. You need to love it to survive it.

— *Where do you look for inspiration?* Day to day, the to do list is never done and doing is its own kind of trap. Creativity needs space and I look for pauses and mental quiet at yoga, meditation and inspiration from reading and drawing. Any kind of travel is a real pause and its own kind of reawakening.

2014 UTS Science and Health Building
The building façade is a monolithic lightweight material, with double layers of offset windows for each floor. The windows vary in size and are arranged in a concertina pattern, swelling and billowing with the building's curving form. Graded coloured reveals, based on the colour works of artist, Gustav Klimt, are reminiscent of a grove of trees.
Photography – Darren Bradley

Free of explanations and annotations, a building must rely on its own eloquence, the eloquence of the physical world. What we see and feel from that direct physical language.

Holman House
Sited on the edge of a 70-metre high cliff, the plan of Holman House refers to Picasso's painting 'The Bather'. It contains a complex series of fluid living spaces set within a meandering perimeter that arcs, folds and stretches in response to sun, landscape and views. Living and dining areas cantilever out over the ocean, allowing dramatic views up and down the coast. The lower floor forms a base that is built from rough stone walls like an extension of the cliff below. These walls continue along the cliff edge to form a series of eccentric terraced gardens and a vase-shaped rock pool.

Photography — Julia Charles

For architects it is an essential refresh, to 'put lead in the pencil', to return to only the pleasure of architecture, free of risk registers, value engineering, fee negotiations and waterproofing.

I am paraphrasing John Berger when he talks about painting but it is true of architecture too: 'a painting has the effect of closing the distance in time between the painting of a picture and one's own act of looking at it. In this special sense all paintings are contemporary. Hence the immediacy of their testimony.' This partly explains the kind of urgency and immediacy that is still palpable in the great works that we visit from any era. We travel in the brilliance of this eternal present seeing and re-seeing the great works. Projects are immediate but never wholly local. They draw on the long literacy of the vocabulary of architecture, the continuum of the language of building, space and type. In the day-to-day practice, great works become the talismen that hold steady in what can be a rollercoaster ride of competing interests and opposing views. Travelling also allows you to see the ordinary anew—a beautiful window, a happy arrangement of rooms, a perfect place for coffee, a sudden sculpture or smoothly beautiful facade. Great cities are there to be seen and read, both their backgrounds and moments, chorus and soloists.

Progressing the profession

There's a real challenge to calibrate our value and rewards to the risks we take and abilities we have. It is too easy to pit architects against each other—we can be ungenerous towards each other. We accept onerous and unfair conditions that work against our value as a profession. It is difficult and time consuming to refute these individually and on a project-by-project basis. We need to work together to reset this, through our professional organisations.

Pencils and pixels

In our office we all draw, measure, write and add up on computer. We all draw and model in three-dimensions on the computer. We all document our buildings for construction on the computer. But these are not the vehicles that short cut the design process or facilitate invention. It is too easy to get lost in a computer; it is both compelling and closed. Architects need to draw on the spot, in three-dimensions and by hand. This is not 'sketching'. These are not necessarily artistic or realistic drawings. They should be incisive, instructive and clear. They are those learned architectural diagrams in action. This is not an old fashioned, bring back the good old days, folksy kind of thinking. Every meeting with a client, builder, consultant group, or other architect is a duel of sorts, sometimes friendly. If you can't draw you are unarmed. This is how you contribute in real time to the messy, iterative, in-the-now process that is called design. Drawing is the only thing builders think they can't do better than you.

Balsa model making is central to our way of working and seeing. Long before a building is built, it is almost fully imagined, living in the models and drawings that describe it. A balsa model is sketchy, iterative and un-precious. It is made and remade, broken and repaired, painted and glossed and then made again. It is not deceptively seductive like a computer rendering. It is not limited to the private space of a personal computer. A balsa model is an object in its own right—it sits out there in the open, open to passing comments, direction and suggestion. A balsa model does not hide its errors or ugliness. It encourages participation, it shortcuts information to a single object, which is ultimately what a building becomes. Free of explanations and annotations, a building must rely on its own eloquence, the eloquence of the physical world. What we see and feel from that direct physical language.

Hannah Tribe

Autonomy and empathy

Hannah Tribe is the founder and principal of TRIBE Studio Architects. A passionate architect, student of literature, art collector, painter, traveller and object designer, Hannah studied at the University of Sydney and then Cornell University before returning to Australia and establishing her own practice more than a decade ago.

3 / 20

TRIBE Studio Architects is widely recognised for its elegant, intelligent and playful built and conceptual work. The practice is now international, and is currently working on projects in Australia, the United Kingdom and the United States. Hannah is also a designer and founding partner of BitPart, a company that designs and manufactures the things that TRIBE can't find for its buildings. In these pages we gain a rare glimpse into her visionary thinking informed by a broad canvas of artistic passions.

Photography — Peter Bennetts

I think all architects need to be polymaths. We need to engage in as many fields of enquiry as we possibly can. My other major interest is literature. I think the love of stories and the study of empathy is a really important part of how we practice architecture.

From the Ground up

My father was an architect so I'd always been surrounded by the practice of architecture, and had holidays looking at architectural wonders. But initially, I never considered architecture as a career. It wasn't until after embarking on a different career that I returned to an architecture degree—because I thought it would be a broad base. I didn't even realise that design was what I wanted to do. So it was more about studying to gain a depth of historical education, theory and philosophical information, and to do some practical work—including drawing.

I studied an undergraduate degree at the University of Sydney with a year on exchange at Cornell. It was extraordinary at Cornell, they have a very strong studio culture and a horrendously cold climate! The combination of those two things, coupled with the strong American work ethic, and their ideals of competition and individualism, leads to the most highly creative environment. I didn't think I would actually ever practise. I never considered architecture as a career. It seemed like something that old men with beards and brown cardigans did, silently, at their desks. Something that looked to me, as a child, like a miserable thing to do. In fact, it wasn't until I had been practicing for about 5 years that I decided I was serious about architecture as my true love. Today at our practice we design all sorts of different things. We do industrial design, architectural design, we draw, we do illustration—it's a broad church.

Starting in practice

It was a great time to be looking when I started out. There were lots of opportunities. So I didn't have any pressure to make any purposeful decisions. I was offered a job and took it, and didn't realise what an amazing opportunity it was. It characterised the 'fresh graduate' experience. Everything looks great and you are completely oblivious to the opportunities you have.

I came back to Sydney and I worked for two practices. One was doing amazingly beautiful and inventive housing and museum projects. The second firm had a more commercial bent. So, in terms of businesses, they were polar opposites.

— *Why did you choose to create your own practice?* I think I've always wanted to have a degree of autonomy. That was quite clear, but the rest of it was all pretty nebulous. The setting up of TRIBE was almost accidental, which is quite embarrassing to admit now.

I didn't like being an employee. I particularly didn't like being an employee with almost no skills. I think the real challenge for graduates is that you come out of university with the most rudimentary architectural tool belt imaginable. This makes the first couple of years of work a real punish. I couldn't see that with any kind of perspective at the time. So I hated having a job, and feeling useless.

I was painting, often on commission, which was great. I had a couple of exhibitions, and I was teaching design at university. Then I started getting small design projects, and then they grew. Now, twelve years later, I am doing that, but bigger.

Chess or bridge?

The real driver for me not continuing my art practice was that as an artist, you need to autonomously and spontaneously create. Whereas with architecture you are given a brief within a set of really tight constraints and within these you can move. It's like the difference between chess and bridge. Both are strategic games that take a lot of intellect and are fabulous to play. With chess you start from the same place every time and you have to drive that autonomously from the beginning. With bridge, you start with a set of circumstances, a dealt hand that creates an element of chance. That takes you to somewhere that you didn't know you were able to go. That's why I love architecture. It challenges me and pushes me creatively to places that within an art practice, I wouldn't be able to set up for myself as a system of constraints.

Beautiful reward

The amazing freedom of architecture is that I get to do something I love every day. So, I don't want to be free from it. The other thing is the experience of having practised as an architect, and now being around my team, I believe if there were anything else that I wanted to do I would be able to skill up and do it.

I have these little highs when I walk into the office. I pause to admire the people that I have collected around me, their talents, and that they are committing a huge part of their lives to making buildings with me. There is that magic that comes out of collaboration; bouncing off people you admire and respect. That is a huge honour and an ongoing delight.

The reality is, the world doesn't want to build things. Materials don't want to get dug out of the ground. People don't want to pay for it. Nobody wants to approve it. Everything's inert and everything is stacked against it. It's such a high when something comes out of the ground. Especially when you demolish something and then it rises again. It's like a phoenix moment, that often comes about by the architect's sheer will power.

House Boone Murray
A 70s renovation has been carefully removed from this 1920s bungalow. The existing house is highly decorative to the street. It is rendered and modelled with some complex corbelling and fretwork. In contrast, the sides of the house are completely utilitarian face brickwork. Framed by irragular openings, the garden views develop a new decorative language for the rear elevation.

Photography — Peter Bennetts

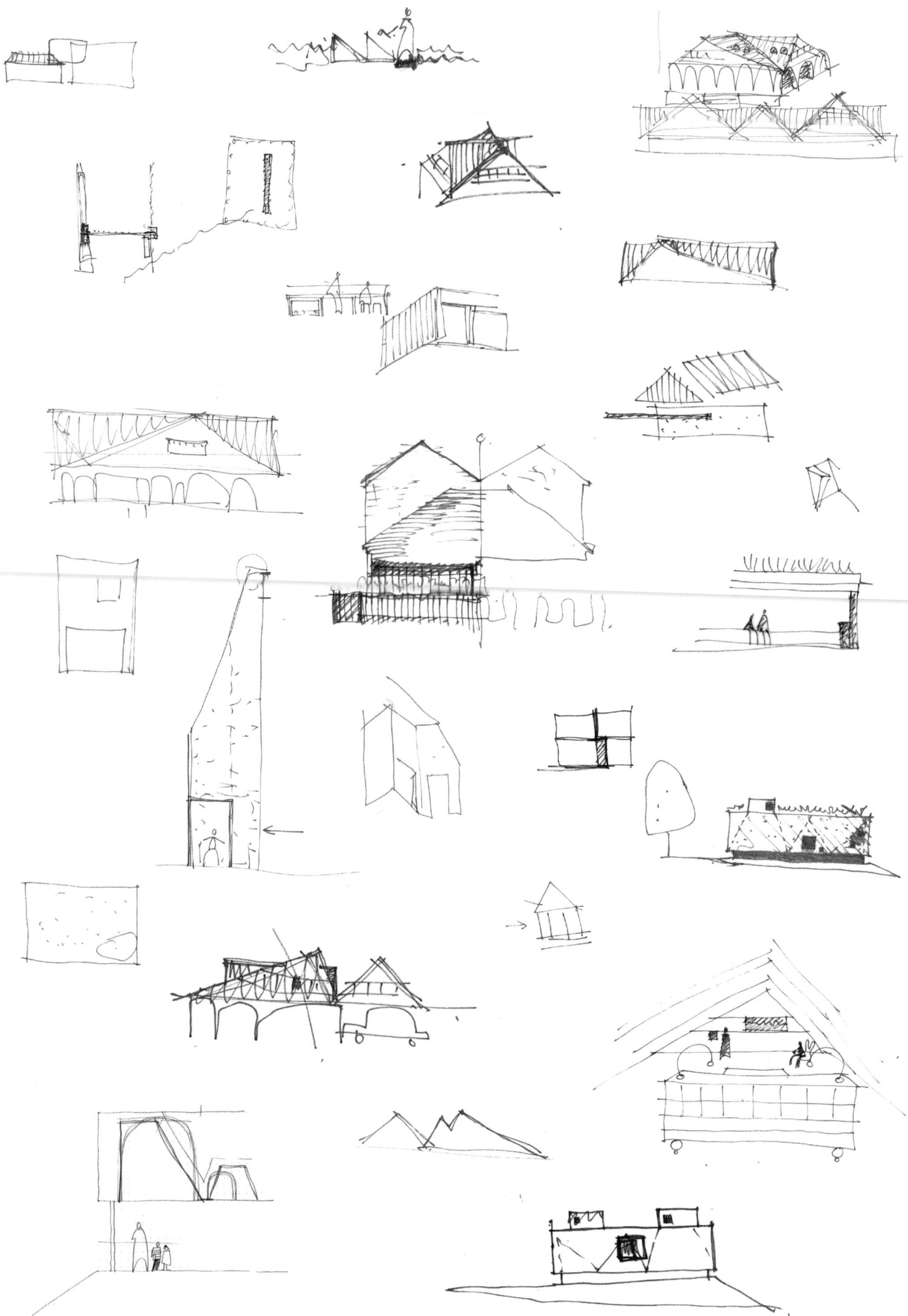

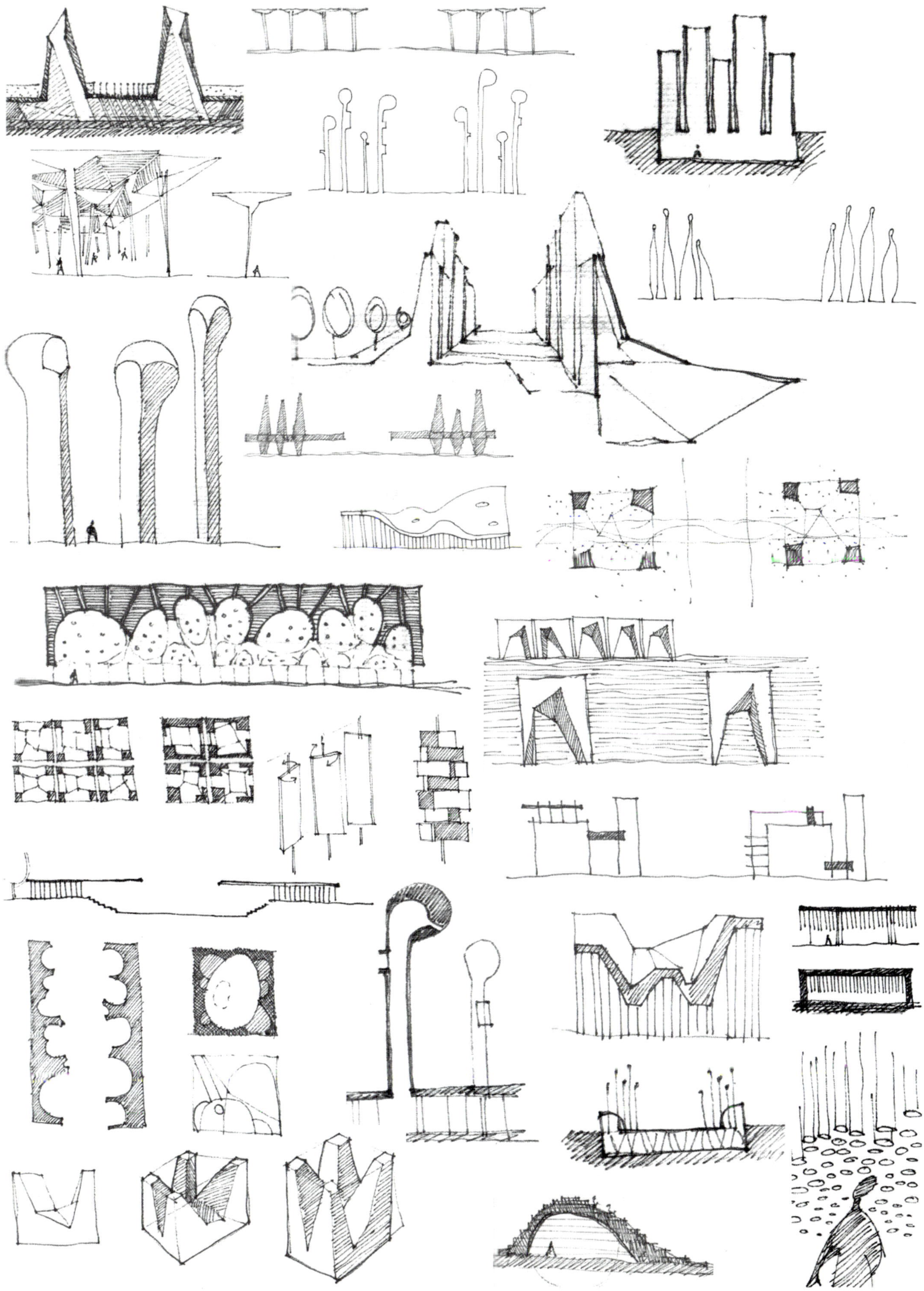

House Chapple
With fantastic harbour views, a northerly orientation to the street-front and a wonderful garden to the rear, the challenge of this house in Mosman is to achieve sun and privacy while appreciating both views. The strategy is a modest one: retain the original 1920s bungalow and carve out new space within its volume.

I think we need to build sustainably, and we need to work ethically. But the days of the architecture being able to save the world, I think that dream is dead.

The result of creating this amazing amount of momentum generated out of the will to push it.

So there is a huge sense of triumph, and relief, when the building finally emerges. It's also a great joy that every project, every building, is something that's come from nothing. It has come through the power of our imaginations, and the passion and the will of an adventurous client. Working with clients is something I really love. I think that comes back again to my love of literature and history. I just love people, with all their eccentricities and difficulties.

Progressing the profession

I'm really sick of hearing architects say that we are not valued as a profession. Well, I say put your fees up. If you don't, you are teaching your clients to undervalue you and take design thinking for granted. That has just got to stop.

As architects we need to better value our time. Culturally, right from university, we expect architects to work all night. We assume they won't do good work unless they are putting in these ridiculous hours. It's a mentality that infects the profession. So we have an expectation of crazy hours being worked, and therefore the fees don't actually reflect the effort put in. I believe this is a huge failing on behalf of the profession. If our job is to provide human spaces, then there is something really fundamentally wrong if we treat our staff in such an inhuman way. I'm very passionate about that. We need to be ethical employers. We should pay overtime to our staff when they work long hours, or not demand they work them. I think that our fees to clients need to reflect this.

Photography — Katherine Lu

— *Is the development process challenging the credibility of architects?* I'm challenged and confused by a conversation I keep hearing in relation to development projects. Where the architects pitch themselves as the 'defender of the city'; their client is the 'bad guy'; and, council is the 'bad guy'. We need to be smarter than that. If you need to protect your projects from a 'bad developer', then don't work with that developer. As architects we can imagine what a project will be like, more than anyone else in the process. So if we really believe that is the wrong thing to do, we've got to stop it and talk about why.

I think we need to build sustainably, and we need to work ethically. But the days of the architecture being able to save the world, I think that dream is dead. Architecture is a very broad church. There will always be architects who were interested in cliché 'monuments to self', you know the 'big fellows' project-type architects that always exist. And so will the 'not-for-profit' architects. I don't know what impact we can have on saving the world. We can certainly work to play our part in doing good. Equally, play a part in not doing any more harm.

Rising above commonplace

— *Does today's education system really measure up?* Architectural education is so broad. At the moment architecture students have to learn an extraordinary amount of technological skills. They need to be able to master CAD programs that are at a level of complexity that was only just imagined when we were studying. To develop that skill set, or that technical competency, within the allotted time means that there are other skills that are not taught to the same level. It's a perennial challenge when you graduate from university, you don't have enough construction knowledge.

— *What advice would you give a student when they hit a brick wall?* I have found one needs to do a minimum of three things a year that make you feel absolutely sick with anxiety. If you don't, you're not growing as an architect. So the brick wall is actually good. It is one of those three things out of the way. I would say, 'just pick yourself up, and keep going.'

This reminds me of a quote from Goethe who said, 'whatever you can do or dream you can, just begin it. Boldness has genius, power and magic in it. Begin it now.' Also a core truth from my pilates instructor, who often says, 'no should, just do.'

— *What qualities do you look for when hiring for your practice?* We particularly look for an open-mindedness about design. Architecture is a harsh trade in terms of design critique. If anybody has any kind of defensiveness around their design process, then they're almost always impossible to work with. So we need to design generously or have a generous design ego. With our young employees we attempt to harness their refreshing naivety, because it's unfettered. An imaginative person with no practical skills will have amazing ideas that you can then get a practical person to deliver.

— *Is there a common DNA running through all successful architects?* No, I don't think so. We are all so different. It's a deliciously varied profession. We each bring a whole bunch of different interests to the table, which inspires our work.

Life Lessons

3

Hannah Tribe

- All architects need to be polymaths
- The best education is as broad as you can get
- Magic comes out of collaboration
- Empathy creates originality
- Always design with generosity
- Do a minimum of three things a year that make you feel absolutely sick with anxiety
- Working with tight briefs gives you freedom to move
- The increasing rise of plurality is liberating design thinking
- Don’t consume architectural images like junk food, savour them
- Architects must place a higher value on their time

Photography — Brett Boardman

House Shmukler
This house is conceived of as a series of boxes suspended in a large shed-like space. The private spaces of the house, the bedrooms and bathrooms, hover over the public spaces. Each bedroom is expressed as a box, pulled apart from its fellows creating a series of double height voids. The edges of the private spaces describe the public volumes.

Radical transformation

The most exciting shift I can see in architecture today is the plurality of architectural approaches in design thinking. In the past there was a very strong binary scene between the 'Melbourne School' and the 'Sydney School'. Now it feels like a really exciting time of architectural exploration and respect and a move away from style into a place of real collegiality, plurality and acceptance.

There's also been a huge shift in the way that we can 'consume' architectural images, much like junk food. We really don't have to understand them and they are not nourishing. They are just kind of fun at the time.

The media has a relentless appetite for content, and that content needs to be really easy to understand. So in a lot of work there is a real triumph of the easily comprehensible diagram, which may or may not make a great project. I don't know, as I haven't looked into them deeply enough, because I am eating my junk food on the internet. Still this 'archiporn' is wonderful in many ways. It means that strong design is accessible for laypersons and architects alike.

In a place like Australia we don't have a strong vernacular so it doesn't matter that we are so internationally influenced. It enhances our sphere of influence. However it does simplify the work, and I'm not sure that's such a great thing.

Pencils and pixels

I'm not a Luddite, quite the opposite. For people who are native in the digital space creating on computers is like drawing for them. It works differently because the extension of their hand is the computer, whereas the potential of my hand is a hand. Technology is absolutely amazing. As with everything the best work comes when you have lots of different people working on a project. With different people, using different tools, you come to a different place. Architecture is such an exciting field to work in. It operates at a strategic political level. It operates at a global and at a national level. At the same time an individual level. We get materials from all over the world. We impact on cities. Even with small design interventions, we are making a huge impact on a larger place.

Architecture is such an exciting field to work in. It operates at a strategic political level. It operates at a global and at a national level. At the same time an individual level. We get materials from all over the world. We impact on cities. Even with small design interventions, we are making a huge impact on a larger place.

Photography — Brett Boardman

Rachel Nolan

Building memory

Rachel Nolan set up her practice with Patrick Kennedy in 1999. Kennedy Nolan has since developed a reputation as a design-focused practice with a distinctive approach to built form. The practice is dedicated to the production of architecture that is highly responsive to its context and seeks to form a strong relationship with landscape.

4 / 20

Design at Kennedy Nolan draws on the optimistic precepts of Modernism empowered by technology. This perpetuates a positive view that the design and arrangement of spaces can support and reinforce relationships, adding piquancy and zest to life. Less tangibly, the practice is compelled to distil the impalpable; to draw on the reaches of memory. Essentially exploring the power of recognising form, colour, texture and light, the resonance of shared memories, of history and landscapes. Here we seek to make more tangible Rachel's desire to make the experience of architecture memorable and meaningful.

Parklane
This is an inner-city house on a long, difficult site that explores what contribution can be made to the urban realm. Abstracted form and civic scale contribute to the lane and small park that flank this site. The magnificent Bluegum towards the rear of the site is the hero of the design.

I would often 'project manage' hide-outs in the bush and down by the river. My best friend and I spent most of our time in a carefully constructed cubby under her house with a floor-to-ceiling height of about 1200mm.

From the ground up

From a young age I was very aware of the environment around me. I enjoyed change and was bossy and determined. Being the eldest of my siblings and sixteen cousins, I would often 'project manage' hideouts in the bush and down by the river. My best friend and I spent most of our time in a carefully constructed cubby under her house with a floor-to-ceiling height of about 1200mm. In the late 1970s I convinced my friend's Dad, Bert, to properly renovate her timber cubby. This involved Bert working the tools to build a new internal wall and the construction of a space-saving hinged table for the 'kitchen'; all in under 6-square metres. Constraints and limitations appealed to me—they still do. Changing, what I could later call 'designing', space gave me a huge kick. I had a taste for it.

Being one of three girls, we were always taught we could do anything boys could do. It was always assumed we would leave home and attend university. I was creative and worked hard and there was something that attracted me to architecture—what I perceived as a 'male' profession. There were no architects in my family and the role models available to me in 1980's film and television were sophisticated Saab drivers, rushing about with large roles of drawings and professional freedom. It's a superficial admission but it looked good from the sidelines.

Learning spaces

At 17 I enrolled in architecture at University of Melbourne. Architecture seemed substantial and useful compared

Photography — Derek Swalwell

to other areas of design. It promised to be an exciting profession that could make a difference and contribute to society. I lived in a residential college on campus for the first two years of my degree. My new home was Newman College, a sandstone building designed by Walter Burley Griffin and Marion Mahoney in 1918. Not just a beautiful building, Newman College is a powerfully memorable building.

This was a building where the architects had a hand in everything from furniture and lighting to the surrounding landscape. Long, low cloisters and dark corridors, set around a central quadrangle supported and enhanced our communal life. Needless to say I was distracted by new freedoms and not very studious. Elements of this place are still powerful memory triggers for me: the smell of lemon scented gums after rain, the warm colours associated with western light, and the feeling you have when you move from dark space into natural light.

When I experience any of these I am transported back to this important building. In second year I met Patrick Kennedy, my business partner and close friend. Newman College affected us in similar ways. It gave Patrick and I common ground to talk about what makes a building or an environment 'memorable'. We talk about this in the work we make together today. We use this language to explain to our clients how our architecture might make them feel.

Starting in practice

I worked in two architecture studios before completing my degree, both were run by women. We drew in pencil, dye-lined prints, hand wrote fee proposals and sometimes smoked at our desks.

I continued to work in small practice after I graduated. Patrick and I lived close by and would often meet for a drink to discuss our day. For graduates we were given a lot of responsibility and were exposed to all aspects of practice. By this time we had a few friends who were keen for us to take on their commissions. So we bit the bullet, resigned, bought a fax and set up our practice in an old shoe factory that I was living in with my partner.

We worked hard but were free and happy. We smoked and drank beer at our drawing boards in the early days; before quickly realising the importance of bringing other architects into our practice.

Patrick and I set up our studio in our late 20s, so we really haven't experienced many other architectural practices. Neither of us had been exposed to issues of gender.

In my personal experience it has never been a disadvantage being a female architect. In fact, when I was younger I was nurtured and supported on site, perhaps even more than my male peers. Tradesmen on site took time to explain and resolve details with me. Maybe if I was a young bloke they may have been keen to make me feel foolish, then again maybe not.

However, there is no doubt that having children changed our practice dynamic. Generally gender in our profession becomes an issue when we have children. It wasn't for me, because I ran my own practice and have a very supportive business partner. Patrick had to step up and run the show, which he did effortlessly. I was eternally guilty and sleep deprived, but determined to not disappear. Many female architects struggle returning to the profession part-

Life Lessons

4

Rachel Nolan

- Distil the impalpable and draw on the reaches of memory
- Design to add piquancy to life
- Do the most with the least
- Take more time to understand the language of landscapes
- Embrace the profession's increasing sense of community
- Champion the social and emotional value of good design
- Your studio culture is as important as the work you produce

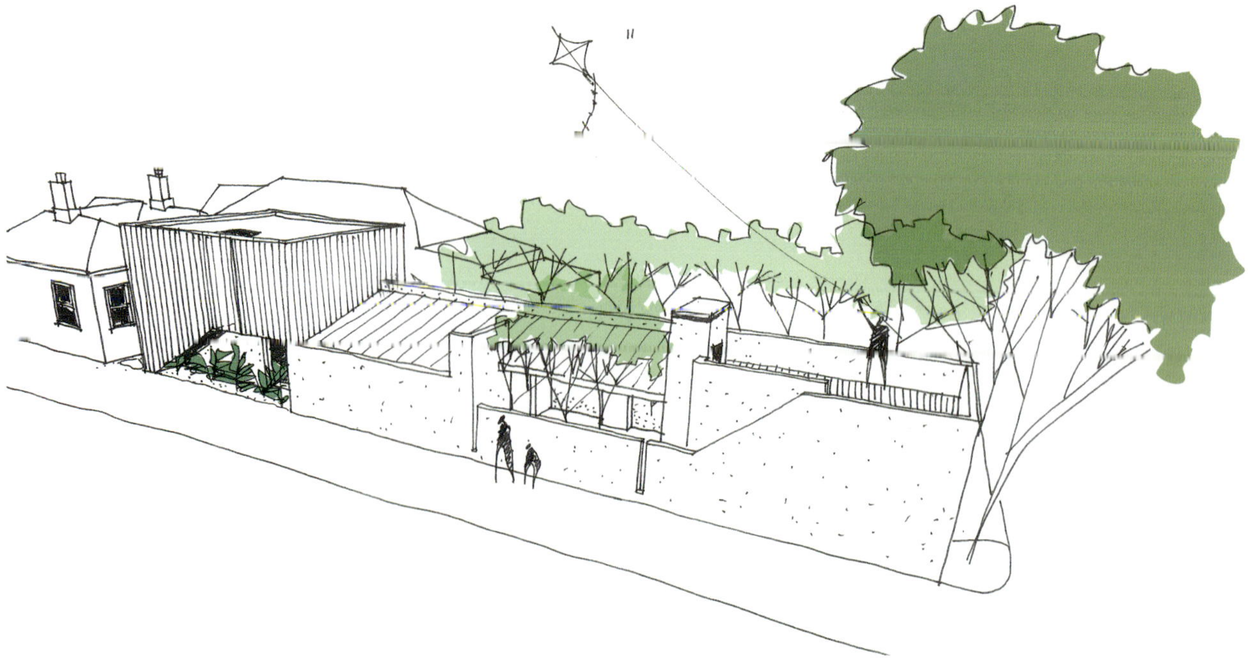

Merricks Beach House
To design for yourself is a real privilege. This is my family's house. This is a weekender, available for short term rent on Mornington Peninsula. It is a small building that is nostalgic yet contemporary. This project continues to make me think about seasonal and temporary habitation. It satisfies my desire to do the most with the least.

time after they have had their children. Within our practice, Patrick and I have always encouraged our staff to return when they are ready and on their own terms. At some point you realise the beauty of running your own practice is that you can make the rules. Babies just became part of the landscape. Since 1999 there have been sixteen babies born to women at Kennedy Nolan. This shared experience and understanding are a part of what our practice has to offer.

Photography — Derek Swalwell

Beautiful reward

Architecture has given me the opportunity to be creative and practical at the same time. It is the synthesis of so many elements. Good architecture benefits from all your life experiences, travel and relationships. There are not many professions that do this. Great enjoyment comes from watching a building come together on site; to see an idea move from the page into its physical form. There are very few quick fix projects in our practice, so it is exciting when we finally get building. It is a long complex affair with so many parties invested in the outcome.

After sixteen years in practice there is now a large body of work to look back on and learn from. In a busy studio it is not always easy to find the space to do this. This opportunity to stop and observe is one we should take more often.

In the early days, design was instinctive. Now we have many projects to reflect on,

We need to advocate for quality over quantity. We need to be inventive and not lazy. We need to make the experience more meaningful.

we have been able to give these instincts words. We are able to articulate our position on how we want our buildings to make you feel. Personally I really enjoy returning to early projects to see how they have settled into the background; to see how they are being used and how the landscape has matured, this is when the full vision is realised.

With the introduction of Instagram into the architectural community we are exposed to more projects during construction. I think this has been a wonderful addition to our profession. Not only does it increase the support and collegiality we have towards each other but it allows the public to understand the complexities of the service we provide—an education if you like. To ensure the progression of our profession, society has to be educated in design. They have to understand its value. They have to understand that architecture isn't just what a building looks like. I believe that this is what it has been reduced to for the average punter, a flipbook of 'looks' or 'vibes'. We need to advocate for quality over quantity. We need to be inventive and not lazy. We need to make the experience more meaningful.

Rising above commonplace

From time to time, we are involved with running design studios at Melbourne School of Design and the University of Melbourne. I would like to see students more engaged with the architecture of their own city. To learn and develop you need to experience good buildings, visit them, use them if you can. There is only so much that can be gained from studying plans and looking at professional photographs. Students need to engage with practising architects in their own town; this is an obvious resource to tap into. Every year each Chapter of the Australian Institute of Architects hosts their awards. Over one or two days architects present their projects to a jury for award consideration. These are open forums where the public can listen to architects speak about their work. They can see real people have to explain why they think their work is deserving of an award and how they visually show this, all in under 10 minutes. They can hear the stories of how long it takes to make good work; how hard it is

Deepdene House
A recently finished house for a family of seven in the eastern suburbs of Melbourne. Much of what Patrick and I have been exploring together over the last sixteen years exists within this project. We are immensely proud of this.

Architecture can be a stressful and isolating practice. Most architects I know work hard. We have to stand up and promote good design and work together as a community.

and how rewarding it can be. Architecture is alive and real in this setting. There is so much for students of architecture to learn from this.

Inspired thinking

To find inspiration ironically I seek sanctuary away from the built environment. I am drawn to big landscapes. Out of the city it is clear to me where my stresses sit in the order of things. My clock gets reset. Often when I return home, I am more interested in the bare essentials—the core ingredients of how to do the most with the least. In my home on the river in Melbourne the focus is more on the garden than the house. Away from work, this balance suits me.

Whilst reading an essay on Robin Boyd by Kerstin Thompson, she introduced me to this quote: 'the object of a design, in architecture as in anything else, is to say or do the essential thing as simply and directly and purely as possible.' I often refer back to this simple commandment.

— *What qualities do you look for when hiring?* There are sixteen people in our studio, including Patrick and I. We think this is a good number, large enough to deliver the projects we are interested in and small enough to maintain the office culture we are determined to protect. Our studio is as important to us as the architecture it produces.

Most of our staff have been with us for many years and are very experienced. In the last few years we have employed a number of graduate architects to even out the ranks. We need our people to be competent and independent. It is also wonderful when we gain team members who are willing to share a part of themselves. Our studio benefits from

Photography — Derek Swalwell

people whose interests are broad, and those who know a sense of humour helps at times.

Radical transformation

In the last five years there has been a far greater sense of community within our profession. Practices are talking to and supporting each other. This is in part due to the culture of our Institute and social media. Our generation of architects experienced a lively studio life when we were at university, particularly in the final two years of our degree. The studio was a space of our own making, and a stage set for high drama (design crits can provoke this). I made close and lasting friendships during my time at University of Melbourne. These friends and peers continue to support me in my working life. I hope the present education system understands the value of this and how it benefits future generations of architects. I am not so sure that certain Facebook or 'virtual' studios are a suitable replacement.

Pencils and pixels

Over the last sixteen years in practice, technology has constantly changed. Things are faster, and undeniably more efficient. Like anything new, we have to work out what suits us and sometimes have had to take a few steps back.

We have found that three-dimensional modeling is a useful design tool within the studio but can be dangerous when in the hands of an overly curious client. We need to educate our clients that good design takes time, that you don't get to see everything at once. It is important that we lead this conversation with words as well as pictures. We need to teach our clients how to trust our design instincts.

Before this technology we would present plans, sometimes elevations and often a few hand sketches for Sketch Design. This was enough to initiate the design process. Good design takes trust. A building needs a certain amount of time to develop and technology has not changed this.

Both Patrick and I still hand draw. He tests and resolves with a thick green pen on layers of butter paper, then he moves quickly into plans on CAD. His ability to move to such resolution at this stage still impresses me. My hand drawing is a little looser and probably more emotive. When I draw I feel like I occupy the building or place; it is a process I can get quite lost in. Often a Sketch Design presentation drawing will be a mash-up of all the technologies we have available to us: a hand drawing over a computer model, with some colour and real folks photo-shopped in. I enjoy this hybrid of past and present technologies.

Recently Jeremy McLeod from Breathe Architecture has had us all thinking hard with the success of his project—The Commons in Brunswick. Jeremy has made apartment life desirable by offering an alternative to the dross that needs 'spin' to sell it. He is currently rallying his community of fellow architects, arming them with information and setting up a model for well-designed high density housing outcomes. He has endless energy and huge faith in his peers.

He is an outstanding supporter of good design and you can feel that his mobilisation of architects has the ability to transform the future of Melbourne housing. Architecture can be a stressful and isolating practice. Most architects I know work hard. We have to stand up and promote good design and work together as a community.

Fairfield

This is project on the Yarra River in Fairfield, is not typically about a habitable building. A number of ‘nodes’ have been designed on this steeply sloped inner-city bush block. One of these is this circular natural swimming pool surrounded by Castlemaine slate and indigenous grasses. The swimming pool uses a Biotop system that uses plants to purify the water.

Photography — Derek Swalwell

Stephanie Little

Fabric of ingenuity

Stephanie Little is a founding partner of Chenchow Little Architects. She graduated in Architecture from the University of New South Wales (UNSW) with honours in 1994. Chenchow Little have received many awards for their work including the Australian Institute of Architects National Robin Boyd Award, the NSW Aaron Bolot Award and the Australian House of the Year.

5 / 20

Stephanie has been involved in each of the practice's award-winning projects, including Freshwater House, Bell-Romero Houses and Skylight House. In 2012 and 2016 Stephanie has been a juror for the NSW Australian Institute of Architects Awards and in 2015 she was a juror for the National Houses Awards.

Materiality and detailing, informed by sensitivity to the larger site context, is a defining feature of Stephanie's practice. Equally, lateral thinking keeps Chenchow Little constantly evolving. Let's get more of a feel for where Stephanie's practically informed aesthetic came from and how it is adding to the rich texture of the built form.

I worked in the shearing shed, mustering sheep and marking for the crop-duster. When I wasn't helping out on the farm, I spent most weekends helping my fashion teacher mum make patterns and sew clothes.

Skylight House
The Skylight House is located in one of Sydney's most difficult Council areas and they really didn't want anything to happen on the site at all. It was a fight from start to finish. Someone once described the architectural process like childbirth. There is a struggle, but when it is over you forget about the process and enjoy the result. This was definitely one of those jobs.
Photography — John Gollings

Photography — Katherine Lu

From the ground up

My parents engaged an architect when I was still in school to design our family home. The project was never realised but I loved the drawings the architect produced. They were hand drawn and beautifully washed in watercolour. I loved how the plans included a place for everything and were a literal blueprint for how we hoped to live our lives.

The influences from my upbringing were full of contrasts and extremes. I grew up on an isolated rural property in western NSW. My father was a third generation farmer and immensely practical.
He was capable of repairing a vital piece of machinery from objects lying around in our shed. Due to our isolation he needed the ability to think laterally to resolve an issue without the ideal machinery part or technical assistance at hand. This way of working has influenced me in my own practice. Having the tenacity to successfully resolve something in less than ideal circumstances and in a short timeframe is crucial to the success of a project particularly with the time demands of a construction site.

As a teenager I helped on the farm along with my mother and sister. I worked in the shearing shed, mustering sheep and marking for the crop-duster. There was no separation of gender roles or limitations on what I was expected to do. We had to make do and get on with the job. My mother studied fashion at East Sydney Technical College. When I wasn't helping out on the farm I spent most weekends helping her make patterns and sew clothes. I learnt a lot about materials, textures and colours from her. How different materials change the way a piece of clothing falls and drapes, and how the patterns had to be modified to suit the chosen material. I saw how one pattern could produce two vastly different aesthetic and functional outcomes depending on the material chosen.

Materiality and detailing have since become important to the work of my practice. Through our detailing we have chosen to manipulate and question the common understanding and reading of the innate qualities of a material.
For example in the semi-detached house the flanges of the structural steel were reduced to the same visual order as the lightweight louvre screens adjacent. This resulted in an abstraction of the facades and provided the building with an effect of weightlessness. We found that the perception of a material could be altered through detailing to create desired effects.

Learning from art

I didn't decide to study architecture until I was required to fill out a university admissions form in my final year at school. My favourite subjects were maths and art. I hoped that architecture would combine the two. I had little exposure to architecture and art other than through books and a wonderful teacher in my school art class. I was particularly fascinated by the work of Claude Monet and his repetitive series of paintings of haystacks and his own garden showing the same view at different times of the day. The environmental impact of the light and seasons completely changed the painting even though the view and composition remained exactly the same.

I later looked at our own work from a similar perspective. Our buildings

Photography — John Gollings

Freshwater House
The design for the Freshwater House fell into place quickly without a great deal of fuss. This image by John Gollings is one of our favourites and has been published extensively around the world. It captures the spirit of the Australian summer, the beachside and the ephemeral quality of the building.

Australian architects are known internationally for their dwellings in a bush setting. We chose instead to focus on housing in a suburban and urban context where the vast majority of Australians live and where we saw a great need for innovation.

are adaptable and changeable for the seasons. Shutters, curtains, walls and glazing can be adjusted by the occupant to maximise the environmental performance of the building resulting in a variable appearance for different climatic conditions. Screens are carefully designed to maximise these effects when lit from the front, above or behind—as the sun moves across the sky. The aesthetic of the building is therefore scripted as much by the environment and the occupant as by the architect.

I moved to the city to study at UNSW when I was 17. In the early years of my course the robust teachings of Professor Peter Kollar were influential. He taught us about the importance of designing for a specific ‘life event’. He argued that ‘Function equals truth and truth equals beauty’. Russell Jack reinforced this belief. He insisted on projects that functioned well and would fail the most beautiful designs if they did not work. This was something that really resonated with me. In practice I have found that there is a common misconception that great aesthetics come at the cost of practicality. We have never seen a separation between the two. The aesthetic of our work is directly tied to its function. A design must work on both levels, or in our view it is not great design. John Gamble was my regular design tutor in the later years of my study. As well as exposing me to the wonderful work of Finnish architect Alvar Aalto, he taught me how to incorporate multiple readings into a design.

This ensured it would function on many levels, both aesthetic and functional. For example, rather than choosing between an open plan or a compartmentalised one, our later projects aimed to be both. We achieved this through a careful consideration of ceiling lines, sliding panels, door openings, built-in furniture, colours and detailing.

— *Was it tougher for women back then?* I was very optimistic when I left university and fervently believed that if you worked hard you would be recognised and rewarded no matter what your background or gender. It wasn't until many years later that I noticed that my female colleagues were not being promoted at the same rate. They were changing career paths and were generally under-represented in the profession, particularly in senior roles. I now believe that their needs to be a conscious effort made to reset the gender balance and organisations such as Parlour are critical to this. Progress has been made but there is still a long way to go.

Starting in practice

Australian architects are known internationally for their dwellings in a bush setting. We chose instead to focus on housing in a suburban and urban context where the vast majority of Australians live and where we saw a great need for innovation. My last year of schooling coincided with ‘Black Monday’ and the subsequent economic crash of the late 1980s. This saw the stock market fall by 40% and the construction sector significantly decline. After my third year of university we were required to complete a six-month architectural work experience as part of our course. There were very few architectural jobs available and the university became a lot more flexible about what it would accept as appropriate experience.

I was lucky to get a job in the drafting office of a large poultry company near my hometown. I worked for several months drafting steel shop drawings for the substantial abattoirs they were building. It was my first exposure to steel construction and the pages of documentation required to build it. The experience—while not architectural—proved to be immensely valuable for the highly detailed steel buildings we have subsequently designed in our office.

After graduation, the recession persisted. There remained very little work for architects and it was not uncommon to see colleagues, given their geographical knowledge from visiting different sites across Sydney, driving taxis for a living. I had worked part-time at a small architecture company through the later years of my course to obtain experience. So when my university friend Tony Chenchow asked me to join him to do a small private job I was happy to accept. Coming from the same university meant that we had a similar understanding of architecture and were sympathetic to each other's views. It turned out that our skills were also complementary, so our practice continued after this one small project and grew from there.

Moments of consequence

Very early in our practice we designed dual occupancy developments. The government had just changed the planning rules to allow another dwelling to be built in the back yard of certain suburban lots in an effort to increase the density of our suburbs. This type of development proved to be very popular with certain landowners (but

Photography — John Gollings

Life Lessons

5

Stephanie Little

- Thinking laterally is at the heart of design ingenuity
- Tenacity is crucial to success
- Work to your strengths
- Learn from architectural precendents
- Sweat the little things
- Great aesthetics shouldn't come at the cost of practicality
- Bring clarity to complexity
- Try different things outside your comfort zone

The Stewart House
The design for the Stewart House sought to create a simple series of well lit spaces, which opened onto the wonderful view of the landscape but were screened from the otherwise bland suburban surroundings. Half-way through the design process the bush-fire codes were amended and we suddenly had to contend with the stringent controls relevant to a flame zone. A lot of work went into seamlessly integrating fire shutters, fire rated roofs and ember screening. Photography — Katherine Lu

Projects extend over years and you need to remain as passionate about the job from day one until completion.

not so popular with their neighbours). We were successful in getting these projects approved by the local planning authority through the detailed analysis of environmental impacts on neighbouring properties and compliance with complex planning codes. To our dismay, once approval was granted the developers saw our role as complete. The developers were intent on building as cheaply and quickly as possible. The government quickly repealed the legislation after a public outcry over the quality of the resulting developments. This experience exposed us to the intricacies of the suburban condition; political involvement, economic forces, environmental challenges, cultural and social influences, copious amounts of legislation, and the passion with which residents guard the amenity of their homes. This informed our critical appraisal of the suburban context and formed the basis of our future residential work. The experience clarified for us where our strengths lay and the type of work we wanted to do. We were eventually acknowledged for our suburban work by Architectural Record in New York and were included in their annual list of ten International Design Vanguard firms in 2010.

After a false start our biggest achievement has been to design a consistent quality of work which we have loved doing. We have put our full passion into each and every project for clients who appreciate the work we do.

Bresic Whitney Hunters Hill
The Bresic Whitney Office in Hunters Hill was envisioned as a townscape set within its tenancy envelope. Independent meeting rooms, workstations and a bathroom core are considered as elemental figures dropped into a container; figures that twist in scale and orientation to create contracting or expanding spaces and guide circulation paths.

Photography — Peter Bennetts

Photography — Peter Bennetts

Freedom to be

Designing a building can be like doing a puzzle. You have to make all the conflicting requirements and components fit together harmoniously. A legal client once compared it to writing a judgement. You have to pull all the disparate strands together to make one coherent logical whole. I love this aspect of architecture. I love when everything works on multiple levels and for me this is its greatest joy and its greatest freedom.

The architecture process is drawn out. There are many points along the way which give you a great sense of achievement; the client's acceptance of the concept, council approval, and commencement of work on site.

After this long and arduous process there is an exhilarating moment when you finally see the form of the building emerge. After it is all over there is almost a sense of loss. You have put so much effort into every fine detail of the project that it is often difficult to let go. That is also the case of your relationship with the client. After working closely together over many years it ends abruptly with the completion of a building. More often than not, we become friends with our clients and continue to see them on a regular basis.

Progressing the profession

Architects need to continually improve their skills and more importantly we need to effectively communicate what our skills are to the public. We need to take on an advocacy role to better educate people of the part architects play in creating wonderful liveable sustainable buildings and cities, so our profession is not undervalued. To achieve this we also need to be realistic about what we are able to do and what we can influence. In most cases an architect's influence is limited. It is wonderful to know that a project can make a small and positive impact on an individual's day-to-day life—anything you are able to achieve beyond that is a real bonus.

— *Do you think the development process is challenging the credibility of architects?* The development process is just another constraint in the practice of architecture and it needs to be treated in the same way as any other.

You can get locked into an image of the building too early. Without the time pressure, BIM has the opposite effect. It can really help you to refine and test ideas like never before.

The Bell Romero Houses
The Bell Romero Houses reinvents the traditional semi-detached house typology for contemporary living. A series of pitched roof forms and outdoor spaces along the buildings length define internal and external spaces and blur the boundaries between inside and out.

You need to fully understand it and work within its limitations. I have always preferred to look at new ways of tackling a given set of circumstances rather than fight head on against them. You have to adapt but remain clear about your objective and what you want to achieve.

Rising above commonplace

Projects extend over years and you need to remain as passionate about the job from day one until completion. I am always inspired by the clear representation of an idea. Often this is in contemporary art rather than in architecture. It could also be in landscape design, film or fashion. I appreciate the beauty, clarity and simplicity of a great idea.

— *What inspires you to rise above humdrum?* After twenty years of working on residential projects, this quotation from dancer Carlos Acosta really resonates with me, 'as an artist, I need to try out different things. You have to evolve, embrace new experiences, learn from them in unfamiliar, unexpected ways. Then take back those different ideas, different tools into what you already know. To learn, to evolve—and still feel, as I do, that there could be even more. I see that as a kind of freedom that can keep you

Photography — Katherine Lu

from repeating yourself. And as an artist, that's one of the hardest challenges. Bringing freshness to what you already know almost too well, so that you don't let it slip into becoming boring.'

— *Do you think the present education system really measures up?* There is continual pressure to reduce contact hours at university and this has had an inevitable impact. Education seems to be less grounded in history, theory and precedent as a result.

Like law, I believe you need to have a good knowledge of architectural precedent and learn how to apply it.

The focus on computerisation makes it too easy for students to create dramatic visualisations of a building without an understanding of the precedents they use, such as how the buildings are put together or how they are planned. On the flip side, their computer skills are a tremendous asset and have changed the way the profession operates.

— *What advice would you give a student when they hit a brick wall?* Students need to discuss their work with colleagues. I find the process of explaining and presenting your design to someone reveals its weaknesses and strengths. When you are forced to verbalise or write down your thoughts you instinctively know which ideas are convincing and which need a lot more work. You can't succeed in architecture without tenacity, persistence and determination.

— *What qualities do you look for when hiring for your practice?* We are very passionate about architecture. So when we hire people we look for that same dedication and commitment to architectural excellence. Passion and perseverance are in some ways more important than experience. We also look for someone who will balance out the skills in our office. Architecture is an increasingly specialised profession. That's why our office is filled with people with different specialities and interests.

Radical transformation

Everything is faster these days. When we started out, the design phase would progress methodically over several months. After a while you would produce a model and some hand-drawn perspectives. A design would evolve out of the process. Everything has now been turned back to front.

A photo-realistic rendering is often expected very early on in a project. With computerisation and BIM we are able to produce these very quickly. So ideas can't develop as they once may have done. You can get locked into an image of the building too early. Without the time pressure, BIM has the opposite effect. It can really help you to refine and test ideas like never before.

Ang House
Architecture is as much about teamwork and managing relationships as it is about design or technical knowledge the client is a critical part of the team. The Ang House was memorable for the delightful clients who have since become good friends. It is one of our smallest projects but with the encouragement of the clients the result became conceptually rich. The clients were so positive and warm and the outcome reflects this.

Tara Veldman

Social architecture

Tara Veldman has experience in design across Australia, Europe, and the Middle East. From early in her career she has had an interest in social architecture; completing her thesis at the University of Melbourne on Cohousing.

6 / 20

In the Netherlands, Tara worked with prominent design firm de Jong Gortemaker Algra on designs for hospitals, mental health and aged care environments. In the Middle East, she also worked as a senior designer for Bluehaus and DesignInc across a variety of complex project typologies. Currently at Billard Leece Partnership (BLP), Tara has been integral in underpinning projects with evidence-based design. In 2011, she launched BLP's Sydney studio and was appointed director in 2014. Tara considers the incorporation of natural daylight, views and nature as hallmarks of her projects. Creating social architecture gives meaning and purpose to her work.

Franeker — Units for Intensive Care
This facility turns the building inside out, providing a covered winter garden at its centre. The small community of clients and staff enjoy coffee in the garden every morning. Communication and socialisation has improved; the residents are less afraid of one another, incidents have de-escalated and all enjoy the material benefits of the building's design.

My sister and I were packed up nearly every weekend and holiday to visit buildings, monuments, galleries, towns and cities. By the time I was ten, I had been touched by the sights and sounds of Europe, America, Australia and Asia.

Photography — Rik Klein

Meaningful places

The contribution of the environment to our life experience is significant in my relationship with architecture. The effect of form, light, space and colour on our existence has played on my intuition from an early age.

During my childhood we lived in a variety of environments. We went from living in an open Australian beachside suburb to the confines of a small, dark apartment in Frankfurt, Germany. Then from this fascinating urban environment, to a spacious house in a leafy park-like environment in Washington DC, United States.

Strong memories of my early travels include my third birthday at an open airy stadium in Seville watching a bullfight with all the glorious colour, harsh noise and violence of the fight. The grand galleries and museums at the Smithsonian Institute in Washington, and the countless presidential monuments that exuded power and formality made an impression on my sense of space. I was even lucky enough to roll Easter Eggs down the White House lawn and ice skate with a chair on the reflection pond in front of the Jefferson Memorial.

The tropical garden paradise of plush Singapore hotels, full of calm, happy people, was in contrast to the flat shells of a small village on Sentosa Island, with the houses built up on stilts above the tidal plain, and the timber room where we shared a local lunch. Equally lasting was the urban experience of inner city

CSP Oesgstgeest
The Centre for Specialist Psychotherapy divided the building into 7 'houses' with lounge and dining spaces on the ground floor, bedrooms above and a private recreation room where the residents can play music or read a book. The views to the forest from each level provide peaceful outlooks and the green sloping roofs ensured the building was integrated into the environment.

Frankfurt and the relief of the green oasis of Tiergarten Frankfurt Zoo. These early travel experiences have shaped the way I approach my life and work. As a result my frame of reference is expansive and my career choices have been made in the pursuit of possibility, to allow me to design spaces that improve the human experience.

Craving creativity

The first years of the architecture course at University of Melbourne were largely focused on practical aspects. Design was the highlight, but the pragmatic construction and technical drawing subjects left me questioning how this actually related to life, emotion and experience.

A Master's degree in set design at University of New South Wales (UNSW) provided the connection to the creative elements of design I craved. We worked with tutors who taught at NIDA, and I was fortunate to obtain work experience at the Sydney Theatre Company (STC). We created physical illusions for the stage, working with light, colour and form to elicit an emotional reaction from the audience. The most wonderful thing was the 'office'—big warehouses on the wharf behind the STC. Here we would slide back the walls on sunny days letting in the light, sounds and smells of the harbour. The impact of the quality of the space on the mood and creativity of the people working there left an indelible impression.

The final two years of my architecture degree were both challenging and satisfying. We explored the social impacts of architecture throughout the centuries. I completed my thesis on 'cohousing', bringing the community back into the planning of these collective housing concepts. The aim being to improve the lives of the inhabitants as well as providing shelter. Professor Graham Brawn and Professor Kim Dovey both had a significant impact on my architectural development and future directions.

I visited the Netherlands and Denmark during my thesis—where the social aspect of architecture is well developed—to research the positive effects of cohousing on peoples' lives. I visited an impressive housing collective for single mothers, featuring small private apartments with common kitchens and living spaces, where paid employment and childcare were managed in a collective sense. At the other end of the spectrum, there was an exclusive terrace house development in the centre of Copenhagen arranged around a communal private 'park', collectively maintained. Seeing these pragmatic solutions, providing the best possible balance of social and personal benefits, intensified my passion to design, first and foremost, for human needs.

After university, I returned to the Netherlands to settle in Rotterdam and explore these 'social' environments further. I also used my time there to indulge my interest in fine art, and enrolled in a fine art degree at Willem de Koning Art Academy. Again I was leaning towards the pure emotional power of colour, light and form. I immersed myself in the ongoing public conversation about the living environment, and the rich history of the variety of living solutions that surrounded me.

Starting in practice

Working with de Jong Gortemaker Algra—a prominent architectural firm—was incredibly inspiring. I started by working on designing interiors. I couldn't speak a word of Dutch so they

Royal Children's Hospital Masterplan
There was significant concern from the local Parkville community about using parkland to build a new large hospital, not least from The Royal Park dog walkers. Our 'park swap' strategy demonstrated that we could not only build a beautiful new hospital within the same footprint as the existing one, but give the land back to the park as well. The dog walkers now call in for a coffee at the hospital's main street with their grandchildren, who play in the garden playground.
Photography — John Gollings

Life Lessons

6

Tara Veldman

- Pursue possibility with a focus on humanity
- Good design moves minds to a better place
- Make your frame of reference as expansive as possible
- There is no right way, architecture is not linear
- We have a responsibility to bring community back into planning
- Every finished project is like making a new friend
- Travel is the lifeblood of creativity
- Immerse yourself in the rich history of living solutions that surround you

'The circulation paths, floating terraces and stairways create movement and offer opportunities for communication'

The residents of the cohousing complex share facilities such as courtyards, gardens, and common areas such as recreation rooms. The journey from city to street, to shared common area, to private dwelling allows residents to determine how and when they interact with the public domain and each other and each area provides space for particular activities to take place there. The social benefits include a sense of community, security and social interaction.

When a project materialises I feel I have made a new friend. It's a feeling of discovery, of recognition and delight.

must have figured I would be more use drawing and designing with coloured texta and fabric! My first projects included mental health and education facilities, hospitals and aged care environments. From concept to completion, my designs started to include buildings specifically for health and rehabilitation. The progressive Dutch protocols giving me the freedom to explore intrinsic uses of space and light.

One of the facilities was The Centre for Specialised Psychotherapy (CSP) in Oegstgeest, a building housing a voluntary assisted-living programme for young adults with eating and personality disorders. The curved, ascending form turned to the forest integrating the bushland into the design. The sloping terraced 'living' roofs looked like an inhabited hill. The focus of the building was to draw the residents to the forest and the light. The project was considered a huge success and people were often found enjoying the sunlight on the terraces facing the forest.

Another favourite was in Franeker, a thirty-bed chronic and acute mental health unit in the Netherlands. The acute mental patients had been living in an old school facility with long corridors where all the rooms were locked at night for safety. In places like these, the scariest thing is often the other inhabitant—being terrified of one another.

The design for the new facility essentially turned it inside out and gave the building a covered winter garden at the centre, surrounded by spokes of living spaces for various categories of client. The residents of each spoke were encouraged toward a central living space by overhead daylight. The central garden beckoned them further and in the end clients and staff were enjoying coffee in the garden together every morning. Communication and socialisation grew and they became less afraid, calmer and happier, incidents de-escalated and the everyday existence of both clients and staff was improved. I returned to Australia in 2002 and began work with BLP—a prominent design firm involved in the multi-residential, healthcare, education and seniors living sectors. This enabled me to pursue my passion for social architecture including the planning of the Royal Melbourne Hospital, the Royal Women's Hospital and the Royal Children's Hospital. Working with Ron Billard, David Leece and Mark Mitchell we brought daylight and nature into our designs.

Again pursuing possibility, I spread my wings to work in Dubai. Working in this hotpot of culture and economics I designed flagship retail stores for upmarket brands, a laboratory building, a hospital in Qatar, and a 'mystery' project where we weren't told the function of the space or what it would be used for—but we lined the walls with lead.

In 2011, I reunited with BLP and established our Sydney office. I started with a laptop and a mobile phone. Thankfully it grew quickly to a small office. Now five years on we have a vibrant inner-city studio and a dedicated team of talented people.

— *Has there been a moment when you felt as if the roof fell in?* Yes, and it's all to do with people. When key members of client teams leave during a project it creates a gap; also when members of my team leave to travel or study the dynamic of the office changes. It's not always as dramatic as the roof falling in but it has an impact every time. Designing a project is a little like putting on a production. If one of the cast or crew leave it creates a space that needs to be filled, it changes the dynamic of the team and the outcome of the project. The project doesn't suffer, it's just different.

Beautiful reward

Design achievement drives me forward. Drawing on a wide variety of opinions and achieving an outcome that responds is uplifting beyond measure. Successful projects take time to design, build and get right. We can standardise and make parts of the process more efficient but in the end it's the process of design that gives our physical environment the attention it deserves. The design outcome should always outweigh the process. Architecture is a universal language where thoughtful design sparks positive reactions. It has given me the opportunity and satisfaction to be directly involved in enhancing people's lives.

As the world changes and evolves, so does the language of design. I feel architects must strive to ensure that our contributions are inspiring as well as functional. Good buildings are complex, challenging to design and laborious to build. An architectural team is part of a multi-dimensional process, translating client vision to a functional application via myriads of details and constraints. Experience, knowledge and creative thinking are essential for successful outcomes. The challenge is achieving an outcome in the most effective and spatially satisfying manner. When a project materialises I feel I have made a new friend. It's a feeling of discovery, of recognition and delight.

Progressing the profession

Good design must be recognised, communicated and valued. In Australia we are becoming more appreciative of the value of the public domain. We have valued this in the past, but currently any sense of social cohesion and community often seems to be overridden in the quest for the greatest profit. We have long understood the value of our own home, but what are we willing to contribute to the value of the greater good?

I hope the future is about ensuring our design response is true and not warped by process, governance, and finances. My inspirational director and mentor in the Netherlands said to me, 'it doesn't matter about the process or the struggle, the thing that counts is the result.'

Wagga Wagga Rural Referral Hospital
With a focus on daylight and views for the patients and staff, the new acute building provides a long awaited new hospital for Wagga Wagga that draws from the surrounding influences of the Riverina and the Murrumbidgee River. The large picture windows in the bedrooms provide an abundance of light and frame the views to the surrounding landscape. The facade shimmers in the daylight like reflections on water and wind through gum leaves.

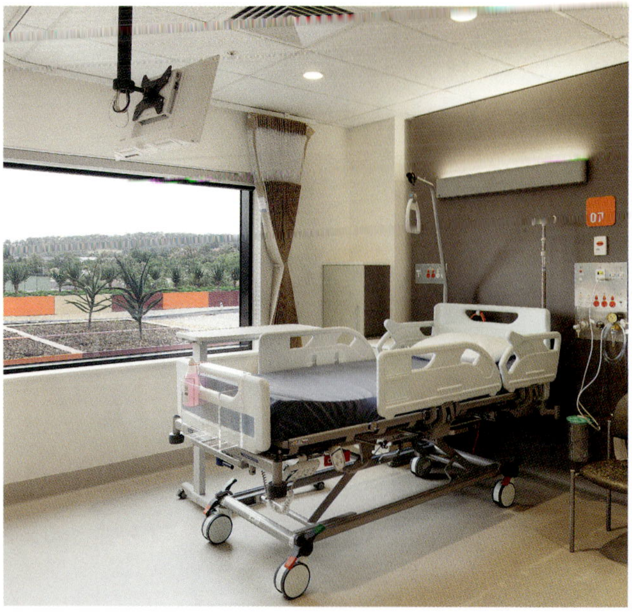

Throughout history, people have built environments that simply provide shelter. Function does not deny good design in fact they are symbiotic. Architecture is both the process and the product of planning, designing and constructing. Living in this era of quick gratification and digital media, brick and mortar remain for a long time. The built-environment has a physical impact on everyone who experiences the space for generations to come.

Rising above commonplace

The experience of the world around us, both natural and built environments, is a constant source of inspiration. It is fascinating to explore the elements that attract us to a particular environment or experience. The challenge in design is to achieve an outcome that encompasses those elements in an effective and spatially satisfying manner.

Inspiration can hit when least expected. Right brain inspiration often occurs when the left brain is dormant. Sometimes a design problem that has been playing on my mind will suddenly resolve itself in the shower—a very right brain activity—or after a long walk or having a coffee looking out over the sea. It's important for my process to analyse a problem then let it settle for a while so the right brain can find its voice.

— *What advice would you give a student when they hit a brick wall?* Change direction, get back to what makes you tick as a person, and look for your role in architecture that is in sync with that. Architecture is like writing or painting, or any other creative pursuit: there is no right way, it's not linear. Keep experimenting, keep playing with the problem. There is always a way that answers a particular spatial problem at a particular moment in time.

— *What qualities do you look for when hiring for your practice?* There needs to be an initial click—someone who 'gets it', of course backed up by the required skills for the position. Skills can be taught or refined. Ultimately finding someone that fits into the team and has the right collaborative work ethic is critical. As the saying goes, 'the whole is greater than the sum of its parts.' Integrity is also important. As architects, we design

Like poetry, books and art, architecture comments upon and documents our multi-dimensional lives.

Photography — Shannon McGrath

spaces for the public, particularly in our community and institutional work. So for me the team needs to have an appreciation that their job is to add quality to the built environment, to create great spaces for the public and the users of the buildings.

Enthusiasm and a willingness to explore new ideas are also key qualities. Design and the opportunities for creating spaces are in constant flux. This makes the continuous desire to solve problems and create solutions an essential part of our practice.

— *Is there a common DNA running through successful architects?*
Architecture is a very broad church, it crosses all scales, contexts and angles. Even the definition of a successful architect is extremely broad. Is it an award-winning architect; one who provides a space that gives the client exactly what they need; or one who designs on budget for a client? Successful architects manage to explain their design and the responses to the question posed. Most significantly they tap into something more—they push the boundaries harder in taking it to a higher level.

Radical transformation

Australia has a relatively short history of building and architecture. We are remote and so removed from large areas in the history of built civilisation. Online information and being able to see an image at the touch of a button has revolutionised the industry, the design space and our lives. This global connectivity and knowledge sharing gives us the potential to go infinitely further. The opportunity to travel has also become more within reach for more people. Providing increased exposure to other cultures and environments creates a new vitality and openness to pursue possibilities.

The ability of architecture to transform the future lies in the ability to respond to the social and cultural ideas of the time. It is inspirational, to describe new ways of thinking about space that capture social and cultural change and manifest it physically implementing the newest technical advances. Like poetry, books and art, architecture comments upon and documents our multi-dimensional lives.

ATM
Telephone

Main Reception
Exit to Edward St

Penny Fuller

Realising potential

Penny Fuller is a founding partner of Silvester Fuller, an emerging architecture studio based in Sydney. Following several years working internationally Penny established her practice with Jad Silvester in 2008.

Prior to establishing Silvester Fuller, Penny and Jad held project leadership and design roles with international architecture studios Herzog & de Meuron (Switzerland), Foster + Partners (UK) and Renzo Piano Building Workshop (Italy). Silvester Fuller's relatively short time as an independent design studio has seen their first built projects being awarded for their creativity in balancing design sensibility and three streams of sustainability, being; social, economic and environmental.

Penny has also been a recipient of the Australian Institute of Architects' Emerging Architect Prize.

Everything is Important—the team at Silvester Fuller is driven by this attitude to find better solutions through the exploration of multiple possibilities and solutions to each design challenge.

Their current projects are diverse and range in scale from product design through to multi-use high-rise developments and cover numerous programme typologies.

7 / 20

Play Pods
Play Pods are the first in a series of design, manufacture and assembly products our studio is exploring. Proof of the power of collaboration, this project was borne out of the creation of our partner fabrication company. Play Pods combine a number of separate functions into a singular object. A series of four bespoke timber pods provide dynamic habitable gathering spaces that incorporate storage display enclosure, seating and lounging.

It's empowering to hold an ability to evaluate complex situations with many inputs, differentiate priorities, and find clarity in confusion through our defined design process.

From the ground up

My mother was always quick to tell me to be the pilot if I played an air hostess, or the doctor if I chose the nurse. I made my little sister play with Lego for hours building towns and cities. My career path was shaped indirectly by a number of experiences, not necessarily any one singular influence. My initial influence would have to be our family home, which is a Pettit and Sevitt from the early 1970's. My parents individually have key traits necessary to be an architect. My mother is very creative and a successful musician. My father is based in the pragmatic, statistical, and logistics-driven field of computer network development. I valued equally these differing influences and approaches growing up. Combined, they seem to be drawn together in the profession of architecture. It was following work experience, during high school, when I decided I definitely wanted to be an architect. My careers teacher told me it was too difficult and that I should choose something easier. Of course this only made me more determined, but perhaps that was her intention all along.

— *What did you learn as an architectural student?* It wasn't important to know everything, that is impossible. However, you need to develop a process to find out what you don't know from day one. In short, be curious, learn quickly and work hard. One of the great things about being an architect is that you are always learning, becoming

Photography — Martin van der Wal

better and better we never stop. Unlike a professional athlete, whose window of opportunity becomes limited with advancing age, architects can be more optimistic about their career path as they mature.

Starting in practice

I was very fortunate to have met some great people during my year out gaining work experience. They gave me an introduction to my first job when I graduated. The job was to work on Aurora Place, designed by Renzo Piano Building Workshop. I was working with the local architect, Group GSA. The job was to start before my final year finished. This was a problem time-wise. But there was no way I was going to let the opportunity slip. It meant a move to Sydney, and a lot of very late nights and weekends spent finishing off my final year project. This is also how I met Jad Silvester, who was working for Renzo Piano on the project at the time. So it was a very fortuitous job to get. I have worked in both large and small practices during my career. I have enjoyed everywhere I have worked and am grateful for the opportunities and experience gained. The decision to start our own practice was certainly not because of lack of opportunity or a desire for more design autonomy. In fact it meant me leaving Foster + Partners in London and Jad leaving Herzog and de Meuron in Basel, Switzerland. It was not a decision we made easily, we had been given great opportunities in both studios. It was at a time when more senior positions were being offered and we both felt it irresponsible to accept such roles if we were not fully committed to stay in Europe. While living and working in different countries had its many advantages, not least the opportunity for travel, the logistics were not sustainable. Having our own studio has always been a desire and this was our opportunity. We continue to collaborate with larger practices and enjoy this very much too. We love to work with great people no matter where they are, how big or small their practice.

Ensuring the roof didn't fall in

From the beginning we have always made sure to only take on projects we know are right for us. By that I mean ensuring we are the right architect for a particular client. Great partnerships are the key to achieving outstanding results. We enjoy building relationships with clients who are interested in seizing new opportunities, willing to grow and embrace the possibilities offered by their project. The evaluation at the beginning is very important and we turn down as many projects as we take. It's all about valuing our design process and having the patience to find those clients who see value in this process. This approach we learnt working in some great studios in Europe and we have successfully applied it to our smaller practice here in Australia. It only works when you allow your studio size to respond to the project opportunities not the other way around.

Beautiful reward

Architecture is more a way of life than a separate job—you never have to stop. Strategising and problem-solving skills are useful in many aspects of life. It's empowering to hold an ability to evaluate complex situations with many inputs, differentiate priorities, and find clarity in confusion through our defined design process. In our studio we have a freethinking culture and are working to be more entrepreneurial. To have the ability to identify and define projects for ourselves, to be proactive rather than reactive is key.

We are motivated by a desire to discover the hidden potential within each project with a resistance to copy or imitate based on stylistic beliefs.

This involves investing time and adopting some project risk. This way we are able to streamline the design to the fabrication process. This gives us more freedom to control the project outcome.

— *What feeling do you get when a project starts to become real?*
There is no point at which a project is not 'real'. There are so many stages in the development of a project all of which are important to achieving the final outcome. What is most exciting however is, through a process of exploration and testing, arriving at the idea that presents the most potential. The point at which we are beginning to 'unlock' the project. It is a feeling of anticipation.

Rising above commonplace

We are motivated by a desire to discover the hidden potential within each project with a resistance to copy or imitate based on stylistic beliefs. Inspiration comes from knowledge: having a solid design process is key. The beginning of the design process excites us. While we consciously don't know where we will arrive, choosing to put aside intuitive responses, we instead allow a rigorous design process to guide us and reveal opportunities within each project. The journey will uncover a unique solution, one that is defined and distinctive while also appearing to complete its context. We believe that it is imperative to

Dapto Anglican Church Auditorium
The first built project for our studio. Encapsulaing liberating thinking, the Dapto Anglican Church Auditorium is the first of a new generation of buildings for the Anglican Community. Devoid of religious motif the project establishes a new church paradigm.

Photography — Martin van der Wal

explore a number of design options. These options are narrowed and developed through a process of review and consultation both internally, with the client, project team and authorities to ultimately reveal the best solution for each project. We enjoy the discussion that occurs during this stage of the design process and believe it is essential for a successful project outcome. Total collaboration is an integral part of our process and is pivotal to deliver an outstanding result. Ultimately, what drives us is the challenge of the problem to be solved. A desire to find the best solution, tailored to each design challenge.

— *Does today's education system really measure up?* There are many differing approaches to architectural education, all of which have their advantages. Traditional architectural education often focuses on providing students with a brief to which they respond. The focus of this approach can tend to be reactive, rather than proactive. In contrast to this, Jad and I developed a masters course at University of Technology Sydney based on nurturing proactive and entrepreneurial thinking in students.

— *What advice would you give a student when they hit a brick wall?* Ensure you have a rational design process and follow it. If you reach a point where you are not sure what to do, go back to your established concept. This will give you all the answers and direction you need. If not, it wasn't clear and strong enough to start with. Most of all, embrace the initial unknown. Don't rush to lock in a solution, be sure to research, understand what this research is telling you and explore from this foundation. Ask yourself: is 'good' good enough? This is something we continually ask ourselves when designing and it pushes us to try harder. Architecture has permanence so you carry a great responsibility to be contributing in a worthwhile way to the built environment. It is necessary to continually question your contribution and it means not slipping into a place of comfort. This question ensures we continually agitate to ensure the best possible outcome.

— *What qualities do you look for when hiring for your practice?* We look for two qualities: talent and attitude. Our team shares the desire to push and test, to make the best possible project out of each opportunity. We look for ability for independent thought and strategic thinking. A willingness to take on any task is equally important. This needs to be coupled with the practicality of driving the many tools we have available to us as designers.

— *Is there a common DNA running through all successful architects?* Successful architecture comes from a place of observation, the ability for independent thought and strategic thinking. It is also necessary to be able to convince others of an idea's merit.

Life Lessons

7

Penny Fuller

- Be curious, learn quickly and work hard
- Take the risk and create your own projects
- Successful architecture comes from a place of observation
- Understand the value that ‘value adding’ brings
- Be proactive rather than reactive
- True collaboration enhances the individuality of the design
- Consciously search for new solutions
- Continually agitate, don’t get comfortable

Destination Table Cape
This concept aims to create a destination that is both embraced locally and known globally. It is a hybrid building: part landscape, part building. The building is an extension of the landscape, sympathetic to its context and responding respectfully to it.

As service industries become more automated, society will become more divided, those who create and those who consume. Architects work continually in the future and need to consider change. Projects take many, many years to be designed, approved and built and need to remain relevant and useful for decades thereafter.

The best project in the world will go nowhere if you are not able to 'sell' it. Great architecture can often be divisive, drawing a great deal of criticism and negative feedback. Determination, ambition and resilience are all essential characteristics to navigate this environment.

Progressing the profession

One of the biggest threats or hindrances to this progression is the current climate of risk aversion. If there is no questioning of previous work there will be no evolution of thought. A desire to progress humanity is a necessary trait in any architect. The progression of humanity relies on strategic thinking and progressive solutions. This progressive thinking should be applied to all facets of society.

Time to draw the line

One of our biggest challenges is managing time pressures. It does not necessarily result in a loss of credibility; this relies on having the foundation of a good design process. However, it does mean that there isn't always time to explore as many options as we would like. It can also lead towards a reliance on a back catalogue of tried and tested ideas. Something we must avoid! Good design can unlock opportunity and is able to add value to a project. Value not only being measured through a project's social or environmental contribution but real monetary value. We select the projects we take on carefully and are progressing with the development of our own; where we can take advantage of the skills we are able to bring to any design problem.

Radical transformation

One of the biggest shifts would have to be in technology available to us. Predominantly within the studio and to a lesser degree on-site. The building industry lags behind the aero and automotive industries for example. Digital fabrication is slowly becoming part of the building process. Within the studio we are exploring and utilising digital fabrication technologies on a number of our own and client-driven projects. Digital fabrication brings many advantages such as less time investment, fewer errors, more efficient use of material, and a generally higher quality end product. The ability to construct more complex forms and ornamentation at little or no additional cost is also very appealing.

Pencils and pixels

During the design stage the computer is one of many tools we employ to explore and test ideas. We rely on physical working models in combination with digital modelling to test design solutions in a workshop environment with our clients and project teams. Parametric modelling has the ability to accelerate and automate tasks that previously would have taken longer. We are able to quickly test the drivers which shape and inform a project outcome whether they be environmental, site specific or brief driven.

The outcome or 'value add' to the project however, is only as good as the input. The drivers must be carefully considered and specific. This approach provides the opportunity to efficiently make adjustments and quickly facilitates the progression of the idea throughout all stages of a project. As service industries become more automated, society will become more divided. Specifically into those who create and those who consume. Architects work continually in the future and need to consider change. Projects take many, many years to be designed, approved and built. Then they need to remain relevant and useful for decades thereafter.

Visualisations — MIR

Sarah Ball

Crafting education

Sarah leads Woods Bagot's Global Education sector. Her passion and leadership across Australia and beyond is exemplified by an extensive architectural and interior design portfolio of successful and innovative projects, many of which having been acknowledged with education and design industry awards.

8 / 20

With broad experience across a range of education environments, Sarah has amassed significant knowledge of; pedagogy; next generation learning spaces, and; technology and academic workplaces, underpinned by her commitment to research. Her core strength lies in the management of complex projects, often with multiple stakeholders. She embraces the opportunity to actively engage clients in the design and planning journey, resulting in an authentic collaborative process that achieves innovative, tailored solutions. Here we capture a little of Sarah's own journey and her passion to enrich learning experiences, through unlocking the full potential of education environments and public spaces.

My childhood was one of exploration, making, doing, and creating. My brother and I were forever making houses out of sheets and chairs. The cubby could be occupied for days on end over the school holidays. The timber top of the outdoor table one day found itself up in the tree in the front garden—high up above the ground we could watch the world go by.

From the ground up

My father is an architect. This still didn't lead to a clear vision as a child that this is what I wanted to do. Nor did he actively encourage me to pursue it. His influence was more that I was exposed to architecture in a way that I might not otherwise have been. I didn't go to site with him, nor do I have a recollection of ever walking around looking at buildings thinking that I wanted to be an architect.

However, I do have distinct memories of my father's study. The A0 drawing board tilted with the slide ruler, set square and the pens. Especially the rolls of drawings—what they kept inside—I loved the theatre of the large drawings being rolled out to reveal something beautiful. The pages intrigued me. The precision of the lines, notations and the composition on the page, to me they were an artwork in themselves. It always came back to the drawings.

As a child I loved to sit and draw. I found comfort in it and still do. Summer holidays were spent with a large pad of thick paper, textas and pencils. The pages would be filled with an eclectic mix of fashion collections and plans of houses. This would lead me to also consider fine arts, fashion or interior design. This is where my father did wield his influence. I started to consider courses that were 'similar' or had an artistic or built environment bent. He was then adamant that I should study architecture first. His argument was that an architecture degree was all encompassing. That it would give me the strongest of foundations and set me off on whatever path I then might choose. My father was right.

Learning space

Leaving school I had no idea what to expect of university or of architecture for that matter. Immediately I was drawn to the University of Melbourne campus; the scale and history represented in its buildings. I marveled at the architecturally significant cloisters of the Old Law Building, Baillieu Library, Wilson Hall, while the concrete lawn was soon a constant hang out spot.

The richness of the buildings on campus compounded the irony for us that the architecture building at this time was possibly the worst building. That said, that ordinary building held so many memories. None more distinct and influential as the studio culture. We all had our own desks from the first year; which I can now look back on as an amazing privilege.

Our final two years were spent together in a small room at the top of the building. No matter what the hour you could be sure that there was someone there. The studio culture gave us the opportunity to engage and get feedback from our peers. This could be helpful at best and also brutal, preparing us for the career ahead.

Starting in practice

I am well aware that my career has been aligned with fortunate timing. When I graduated in 2002, the economy was strong and there was no issue in finding jobs in Melbourne, or even abroad for that matter. Upon graduating, I was offered a permanent position at the firm I had been working at part-time through my studies.

Deakin University Burwood Highway Frontage Building (Building BC)
The architectural intention centred around two key concepts: the spatial composition required by the functional brief, and the client's aspiration to create a gateway building for the campus. Our approach was to orient the building away from the southern edge and the highway, creating two north-facing courtyards that act as social gathering spaces for the public and university community, while also reinforcing and extending the landscape nature of the Burwood campus. The process enabled us to work with the university to consider the interior as a new academic workplace that is more akin to a contemporary workplace environment than a traditional, cellular layout.

Photography — Peter Bennetts

Life Lessons

8

Sarah Ball

— An architectural eye gives you the freedom to question everything

— Delve deeper into how design can affect people on a personal level

— Sometimes when things appear to be falling apart they may actually be falling into place

— We have a huge responsibility to free people's minds and enrich their lives

— A collaborative studio culture is absolutely crucial to success

— Connectivity through technology is as invasive as it is liberating

— Championing the real value of good design is essential and can't be underestimated

— Reality DIY television shows are undermining the credibility of design

DEAKIN
DEAKIN UNIVERSITY
DEAKIN
Worldly

Photography — Peter Bennetts

Victoria University Student-Led
Inter-professional Education in Health
The design was uniquely tailored to the clinic's innovative approach to inter-professional education and health care, while the built form references the unique landscape of Werribee in a U-shaped form. We delved into understanding how design can impact on a patient's experience and the history of the local Werribee area. As such the design aims to not only reflect the unique health service offering but to provide a sense of community beyond that of a traditional health facility.

With almost a year under my belt, I packed my suitcase to become a graduate architect at a large multidisciplinary firm in London.

London was booming and the government had made a significant commitment to education; including building works for new schools across the country. Eager to learn I had no idea what education and architecture could entail, but it pricked an interest and passion that I did not expect.

Never one to sit back, I requested a lead role within the larger team and soon found myself attending meetings with principals and teachers; discussing how the design space needed to respond to and enable the learning experience. This experience would take me to a similar role at Wilkinson Eyre Architects. It was a brilliant place to work. The support of directors and leadership cannot go unacknowledged. I still keep in contact with Stafford Critchlow [Wilkinson Eyre director] today. He empowered me as a young graduate to ask questions and challenge the constraints put in front of me and was always open to my ideas.

I returned to Melbourne and Woods Bagot, where I still find myself today. I became a partner at Woods Bagot in September 2008. There is no ambiguity in the date for me, as it coincided with the Global Financial Crisis (GFC) and all of the decisions that as a business owner went with it. Projects went on hold indefinitely or were cancelled. To make matters worse it also aligned with large-scale projects such as the Melbourne Convention & Exhibition Centre coming to an end. Decisions had to be made and delivered. There simply wasn't the work. I was conscious that even as we were saying goodbye to a good number of our

Photography — Peter Bennetts

staff, that there would be a whole fresh breed of eager graduates about to step into the world with realistically not enough opportunities to support them all.

Beautiful reward

I take great joy in the people that I work with. Many of which have become lifelong friends. Working in a large global practice has also afforded me the opportunity to work with so many talented individuals that are truly inspiring. We also have a great team in our Melbourne studio we have built up over the years that certainly makes it a pleasure to come to work each day.

I truly love working in the education sector and creating spaces that enhance the student experience. There are so many brilliant teachers and academics doing amazing things with limited resources and sub-standard spaces, but they still have this desire to create something unique and have a powerful impact on students' lives. The fact that we can then be involved to create spaces for them that meet their needs and provide architecture that inspires and enables—rather than limiting their imagination—is highly rewarding.

Making goose bumps real

The moments of visiting site and realising the drawing come to life is like an injection of pure wonderment. It goes beyond just the physical realisation of if it looks exactly how you hoped it would. It is more a feeling of place—it gives me goose bumps.

One of my first projects I saw come to fruition was the refurbishment of the Old Engineering Library at University of Melbourne into a new student learning centre. I remember walking through the project as it emerged and finally when it was completed. I find there is a calmness about being able to walk through a space by myself at first and take it all in. Just to explore and notice all aspects of the architecture. On the flip side, there was this great injection of energy seeing students arrive, making the space their own and using it as I had hoped—or even in ways that I hadn't anticipated or imagined.

This highlights the fact that architecture has given me the freedom to look at the world through a different lens. The opportunity to explore the world and soak it all up. I love nothing more than exploring our cities or local suburban streets. Observing how people are going about their everyday lives and are using public and private space.

Photography — Michael Downes

The rise of the realist DIY television shows where everyone is a designer and the developer knows best, undermines the value of the architect.

On the grander scale it has given me the freedom to marvel at incredible cities of different scales across the globe. Good design makes my heart sing when it brings people together.
Bad design just makes me angry in the way that it can impact negatively on the development of our society. In essence architecture has given me the freedom to question everything.

Progressing the profession

There are many issues to tackle to ensure the progression of the architectural profession; the value of good design stands out for me. If the broader industry (clients and the community) see the value in good design then I feel a number of other issues will also be addressed.
How we do this I am not entirely sure as there is plenty of evidence that good design makes economic sense, but architecture and design is increasingly questioned across all typologies. We need to continue to advocate for this at a government level.

Realising true value

Architects fees are often subject to intense commercial pressure.
As a profession we need to continue to advocate that our fees are reasonable. They represent a small fraction of total construction costs and are even smaller (less than 1%) when considered against the whole-of-life cost of a building. Good design is an investment that generates true value for money.

Good design also takes time. Time to think, explore, test and develop ideas. With the world getting quicker and people wanting things yesterday, clients are often being advised that projects can be crunched by getting contractors involved earlier to manage risk. But what risk is it managing? Yes it may give the client some more certainty in meeting an end date and budget, but little more. We are increasingly seeing projects tendered earlier and earlier in the design process with the expectation that the design is resolved and everything covered.
It is simply not possible and it only goes further to devalue the role of the architect and the value of good design.

There are clients who see the value of design in their development; these are the ones who we want to keep working with. They are committed to quality design and the value that the architect can bring to this.

Progressing humanity

I think that there has always been a commitment to progressing humanity in architects, both young and old. However, young architects are more connected than ever before to all of the issues confronting the world; mass migration, urban sprawl, developing nations, the imagination of the cities both new and old. As a profession, it is incredibly important that we are committed and leading the discourse on how sustainable design and development of the built environment can make a significant impact on the progression of humanity.

Rising above commonplace

— *Do you think the present education system really measures up?* Having hired some brilliantly talented and diverse graduates over the past years I would be inclined to say to a certain extent yes. They have all come from different architecture schools. However, whether it is due to the education system or the traits and drive of the individual would have to be questioned.

Ruyton Girls School, Margaret McRea Building
The New Margaret McRea Building supports Ruyton Girls' School curriculum approach to inquiry-based learning that exemplified the shift toward student centredness. The challenge was to create an innovative new architecture that responded to the history of the site and specifically the iconic Henty House. The fluid plan and organic form formally embraces and celebrates this central gathering space for students.

I believe that it is our responsibility as architects to be truly aspirational. We must strive for creative responses that challenge the status quo. For me outstanding architecture has to be timeless, beautifully crafted and conceptually rigorous.

Photography — Michael Downes

Commonalities between the graduates that should continue to be encouraged through the education system is the ability to think laterally, to be proactive, to push boundaries, to engage, to be inquisitive and explore.

At the time when I studied, University of Melbourne required you to take a year off between your first Bachelor degree and the final two years of architecture. In that year you had to work in an architectural practice for at least six months.

Eager to make the most of the year out, I worked my six months to the day and then backpacked for the next six months around Europe with one of my closest friends, who I met on day one of architecture orientation.

A long list of projects would define our travels where we would navigate regional trains to the Bauhaus in Dessau, make the pilgrimage to Le Corbusier's chapel at Ronchamp, marvel at the facade of the Jean Nouvel's Institut du Monde Arabe, stand in the incredible Pantheon and truly understand the uniqueness of the Antoni Gaudi's projects throughout Barcelona. This is where all of the slides in lectures and pages of books really came to life for us. We could begin to understand the power of architecture at such a scale.

While some may be eager to get through their course in the quickest amount of time, this year out provided time to reflect, explore and engage with all that we had been taught to date. I would also say that my years of study were much richer for it.

Photography — Michael Downes

—— *What advice would you give a student when they hit a brick wall?* Breathe, architecture can be all consuming and you will hit many walls along the way —some that can seem insurmountable. You have to remember that you are not alone and that there is always a solution to a problem. It is important to have a network of like-minded friends to bounce ideas off. Don't be afraid to share your ideas and get feedback or even ask for help. I remember when we were studying that some people would keep their work secret, only to reveal it after an assignment had been submitted or it was time for the final design crit. They were worried that someone would 'copy' their work or idea. But what I found, from working in the studio environment and getting feedback from fellow colleagues, meant that I would have to be very clear with my design concept through every stage and could move beyond each hurdle as they arose as opposed to letting it build up into one huge insurmountable brick wall.

One lesson that I continue to wrestle with is that you can't control everything and that if you try not to cling too tightly to the outcome that things will work out. A project lost may free you up to focus on something else that may turn out to be even better. A change in client brief may open up a solution that you hadn't thought of. Sometimes when things appear to be falling apart they may actually be falling into place.

—— *What qualities do you look for when hiring for your practice?* Being a large studio we are often looking for architects with a wide range of skill sets and experience. For me a sense of design and passion for architecture and the built environment are a given. Depending on their level of experience we will also be looking for their potential to grow and take on more leadership responsibilities. It certainly doesn't mean that we looking for all of our staff to be the same. What is important though is that they are all part of the team culture and aligned with the ethos and aspirations of the practice. Commitment and eagerness to learn are important and I think if you have that in your staff and a cultural alignment you are setting the framework for a great studio and the projects.

Radical transformation

Connectivity is by far the most radical shift I've seen since starting out. I remember as a student working part time in a large architectural firm and there would be a few times a day that the faxes were handed out to everyone. There was no email. There was time between responses. Time to do work. Time to consider possibilities and explore ideas. Today we are infinitely connected with email and mobile. Clients, consultants, and colleagues all expect you to be available at any time. It can be completely invasive. Responses are expected instantaneously and there seems to be a loss of appreciation for the time that is required for the design and documentation process.

At the same time we are connected to the design community all over the world. We have more and more information available, the ability to engage with architectural design and projects as they are designed and developed. The ideas and learning that can be tapped into are more available than ever before.
This provides the ability to work across studios with people all over the world. This is the core foundation of the intimate, yet global scale of own studio culture.
In essence, our studio is like a large co-working space that you could consider as groups of small practices. The size of the studio enables us to engage and influence design and communities at a scale I could never have imagined.

Debbie Ryan

Unrelinquished passion

Debbie Ryan is an owner of McBride Charles Ryan with vast experience in the design of commercial, institutional and domestic projects. Her scientific and intuitive design abilities, acute sense of composition and extensive product knowledge has given her a wide and renowed reputation.

9 / 20

Debbie's work has been widely published and she has gained recognition as a public speaker and critic of design and architecture. Debbie's practice has also won numerous awards including World Architecture Awards for the Klein Bottle House, Fitzroy High School and Monaco House.

She believes that architecture should never relinquish experimentation, and uses architecture of all scales as a means to this end. With forms, spaces, materials and context all up for grabs, Debbie explores every dimension to reinvent places and create new possibilities.

I still can smell our trips to the city. We would stay at Victoria Hotel in Little Collins Street. It was exciting, I remember the foyer and sensed the age of the building and that part of the city.

Dome House
A home in Hawthorn designed to accommodate the various stages of life: a family, a single person, and a single person with large visiting family. In this project, the copper clad sphere is partially buried, and then eroded internally, and at on the north and south sides to create two different gardens. The central ground floor space is detailed as a continuation of the exterior gardens, and all other spaces are either arched over or dispersed around this main space.

Photography — John Gollings

As a young person I was exposed to many different architectural environments. Due to the nature of my father's work, our family was constantly on the move. I can count 15 houses in 3 states by the time I reached 13 years of age. I have a photographic memory of each new house. Each had its own individual character. In Whyalla we had a stone house made of big blocks. It had velvet curtains that divided the lounge from the hallway. We held performances there. It had violets in the frontyard and an enormous backyard, which went on forever.

Renmark was a mean house, made of asbestos probably, and its only redeeming feature was its proximity to a weighbridge where we would take a bucket and get it filled with stone fruit or grapes. There was a large front lawn where we would run under the sprinkler—it was hot. I also remember our house in Shepparton—our introduction to the modern speculative house. I remember the school in Burnside, Adelaide; an experimental school with Sea Grass matting and operable walls. The differences in housing and schools are still vivid memories. Even if nothing else is, I was acutely aware of my environment.

My mother was a dressmaker and eventually my family business was in Manchester. Our new house, fabric patterns, colour and texture were all topics of contemplation and discussion. So perhaps it was this combination that laid the seeds of interest in design. At school and university I was initially attracted to art studies. It was while studying fine arts under Patrick McCaughey at Monash University that I really became aware of architecture as an art and I was enthralled and excited by it. I introduced my partner to the lectures and he too was captivated by them. That year we both decided to swap courses, Robert [McBride] to RMIT Architecture and I to RMIT Interior Design.

I studied fine arts and interior design. I could have focused on interior design, which I did initially. Architecture, even when I was a student, seemed to have more rigour; like any art it needs a reason or a theory for being. But in a funny sort of way that interest in fabric, its texture, colour, and the way it folds has influenced the architecture we produce. I think our work intersects! I met some great teachers at RMIT. Clare Newton, an architect teacher, is one who has remained a supportive friend. I spent most of my time observing or participating with the architecture students. I shared a studio in Little Bourke Street with only architecture students. That course was then heavily influenced by Peter Corrigan. If there was a simple lesson that I could take away it would be—be bold.

— *Was it tougher for women back then or was it a non-issue?* I think coming in at the bottom is not a problem. It is when the stakes are higher that things become harder. When you are doing small jobs no one blinks—when you are doing large jobs that's when discrimination really kicks in. Then the 'boys club' mentality becomes clearly evident. It's tough at the top and competition is fierce.

Pegs Infinity Centre
The key quality of the infinity symbol is its connectivity; a recognisable topology that allows its meaning to withstand formal deformation. This flexibility is evident in the manner with which the building occupies its awkward L-shaped site while joining all the disciplines and environments to provide a rich and seamless experience for staff and students.

Finally there's that short-lived moment of hubris. When it is actually pretty much as you had hoped and when you think you're the ant's pants.

Starting in practice

I have always worked for myself. I have this pretty independent streak; I just wanted to run my own show.
I think I would be an awkward fit in a big hierarchical corporation.

We started in 1988—they were heady days. Anyone who had a scrap of talent could get a job. I had a lot of freelance work, which I did from the studio in Little Bourke Street. I had so much that I got Rob [McBride] and Tony Charles to help me. I said we should have our own business. We started in Rob's and my apartment. Representatives had 200 steps to climb with samples. We quickly found a basic office in Queensberry Street, Carlton with 100mm of pigeon droppings on the floor. The building had a tin roof and it was hotter inside than outside on a hot day. In winter we virtually sat on our individual heaters. We would also be greeted every morning by a layer of dust from the road outside on our drawings.

I started by designing sets for exhibitions and photographic shoots. In the early days, I supplemented this with sub-contract work for people like Ian McDougall (ARM). Slowly, very slowly, we graduated to real work such as cafes, small houses, and extensions. Pretty typical really—nothing much changes.

In terms of life and work balance I have been luckier than most. After Queensberry Street, I have always worked very close to home. We designed a 10-unit development where we lived in one and worked from another. More recently we designed a building where the home faces the street and the office faces the back lane with a courtyard in between.
I have not been far away from my children since these moves. We have had some instances when we have been trying to have a serious professional client meeting and children have decided to bounce a ball very loudly outside the room —such is life.

Moments of consequence

In the early days the recession hit us hard. The roof collapsed slowly, you barely noticed. Until one day you realised there was nothing and it was almost too late to do anything about it. Then there was the time my partner Robert was forced to take a long break from the business.
This coincided with a lull in work, my eldest child in VCE, and the construction of our house and studio. Everything at once. Life goes on somehow. You just grind it out and if you stick to your guns you pop out the other end.

Beautiful reward

We've also had our fair share of highs on the journey. Just doing the Dome House and the Klein Bottle House—especially presenting it at the World Architecture Awards and it winning! Seeing the Victorian Comprehensive Cancer Centre and the Quays at the Docklands through to the end are other significant milestones. The school work for PEGS, Fitzroy High School, Dallas and Ivanhoe Grammar also stand out. Most importantly the greatest reward is just hanging in there doing buildings that we like. Buildings we think make a contribution to culture and people.

Architecture also certainly frees you from boredom. Despite the many negatives that plague the profession, my working day is hardly ever dull. Doing buildings particularly of the public variety is an enormous privilege. You are impacting, and hopefully improving, the world in a very physical way—I believe this is a type of freedom. Then there's the thrill of winning the job. That's a victory for a start, and the warm sense of security it brings. Followed shortly by the terrifying responsibility of actually doing something that is good and original—a period which is a bit like holding your breath until finally something of value emerges. Then the long haul to bring that idea home.

It is of course extremely rewarding when the landscape and the object have a synergy. Nature too has some wonderful lessons in colour, pattern, form and geometry but I would not necessarily rate it all higher than a meaningful response to culture and ideas. Finally there's that short-lived moment of hubris. When it is actually pretty much as you had hoped and when you think you're the ant's pants.

Progressing the profession

I think the criteria for selecting architects on projects is often skewed too much towards the fee. If clients actually compared the money they are saving on the fee against the potential for a design service that is inevitably compromised by that, then they would rate that aspect of an architect's submission, significantly lower. Ever year the fees are lower and this is coupled by increasing responsibilities, and more onerous contracts. It's difficult to know what will arrest this. I think it is one of the reasons why there are so few young firms participating in the public sphere.

I do not want to sound like the disgruntled old guard but I do worry a bit about ideas and aesthetics in architecture. This is not universal of course, but there appears as if there is a recoiling in the profession from the hope in the potential of what architecture can mean and represent—in its ambition. It could be that the younger generation have decided it's too hard or perhaps they are just biding their time. If their work is a reaction to a previous generation then that is a good thing. However, I haven't heard many articulate what the nature of that reaction is. There is no new proposition and because of this I wonder if it has lost its way.

The rush for development at all costs is also subverting the credibility of architecture. Just check out Melbourne's skyline. Architects on the whole are well intentioned. Through the processes that bring about large development—while they are the last to relent—they almost inevitably get dragged

Photography — John Gollings

Photography — John Gollings

Ivanhoe Grammar Senior Years & Science Centre
The key characteristics of the learning spaces were transparency, variety of spatial type, multiple-use, flexibility, adaptability, and interconnectivity between the learning spaces and the outside environment. The angular internal geometry contrasts with the building's circular shape, highlighting entry points and providing a distinction between the outerworld (singular, circular, muted landscape palate) and the inner world (complex, expressive & colourful).

Politically, socially and culturally architecture is still not appreciated enough. The newspapers can be scratching for a story but still not cover architecture.

Photography — John Gollings

Photography — John Gollings

into accepting standards they are not happy with. I don't think government and authorities have the processes in place that they should to prevent this. When you get a good result there is almost always some unusual strong willed individual on the client side championing you or the design; someone essential standing up to the pull of mediocrity that our processes for procurement bring about.

Gender parity

Certainly women remain disproportionally represented at senior levels of architectural firms on the lower side. The quality of female graduates, the prominence of younger small practices run by women, and the active stance of organisations such as Parlour suggest that this though is heading in the right direction. Politically, socially and culturally architecture is still not appreciated enough. The newspapers can be scratching for a story but still not cover architecture.

Rising above commonplace

Experiencing as many buildings as possible is essential. However a good written interpretation of a piece of architecture is a wondrous thing. Knowledge is inspiration. I generally find this in the history and tradition of architecture, modern and contemporary art, mathematics and geometry. Also the ordinary stuff, the undersigned stuff that surrounds us.

— *Does the present education system really measure up?* We have active links with RMIT, Monash, University of Melbourne, and Deakin University. The passion from the good students and commitment of the teaching staff is very high and on the whole it's impressive. Like all professionals I do on occasion want for more practical experience but that is not really the point of their education. I do sometimes think there could be a kind of general subject that prepares them for work, talks about the processes, warns them of dangers and gives them priorities in way that a single topic subject does not. I think if done well it would empower them. Students need to understand business; if they don't make money they can't continue to operate.

Progressing humanity

Architects are particularly prone to thinking that they can change humanity through design. Like most in the western world we all suffer from the guilt of our stroke of goddam luck. I prefer political activism to insignificant feel good actions that simply anaesthetise that guilt and distract us from the bigger issues at hand.

Radical transformation

We started when Postmodernism was hitting its straps. From that obsession with the language of architecture and its traditions there has been very radical formal invention in architecture: an attempt at fulfilling the promise of the Constructivists in the 1920s. Some of this has been kicked along by the increased use of software. Since then, there has been an increased obsession with the materiality of architecture, in its expressive and textual potentials. I think our work intersects with all these trends without fitting fully into any one of them. We are interested in the language of architecture, and the use of texture and materiality to bring vibrancy to that language. Yet, clearly we are equally obsessed by experimental form in architecture.

Architecture can also be a symbol of what's possible and an antidote to the mundane. I don't think it's too utopian to consider that transformative.

Victorian Comprehensive Cancer Centre
MCR partnered with STHDI as part of the Plenary consortium winning bid
The Victorian Comprehensive Cancer Centre (VCCC) Project is delivering a new $1billion facility purpose-built for cancer research, treatment, education and care in the Melbourne suburb of Parkville, Victoria. In addition to the new facilities being built, ten world-leading cancer organisations have come together to form the VCCC Alliance to share knowledge and resources and drive the next generation of cancer research, education, treatment and care.

Photography — Peter Bennetts

Pencils and pixels

At MCR we like the thrill of reinvention. We have enjoyed exploiting the potential of digital design for many years.
It has certainly opened up space for us to work. We have found it a way to test ideas quickly. It can however on occasion deceive you, distracting you from the physicality of the thing you are producing. As we have grown older we understand better the benefits and limitations of various programs. There is no one piece of software that serves us, we are now better at using the suite of programs available to maximise the result. Undeniably careful, sensible culturally responsive development clearly has amenity benefits. Our cities are simply better more vibrant places to be because of it.

This is not really dependent on expressive architecture or architecture as an idea. The architecture that we do seeks to bring another layer of vibrancy and vividness to our cities. I think the 'Bilbao Effect' is real and not dependant on mega-budgets and mega-architects but can (and does) happen at a micro level everywhere. Architecture can amplify and give identity to our institutions, those places that harbour our values as a society. Architecture can also be a symbol of what's possible and an antidote to the mundane.
I don't think it's too utopian to consider that transformative.

Life Lessons

9

Debbie Ryan

- Success demands an eye for beauty and good communication
- Challenge the mediocrity procurement processes can bring
- The ‘Bilbao Effect’ can happen at a micro level everywhere
- Be both scientific and intuitive
- Architecture and interior design should be indivisible
- Embrace all scales and never relinquish experimentation
- Make your work an antidote to the mundane
- Simply be bold

Rachel Neeson

Adventurous ambition

Rachel Neeson studied architecture at the University of Sydney, graduating with the University Medal in 1993, and completed a Masters of Architecture in Barcelona. She formed Neeson Murcutt Architects with her late partner Nicholas Murcutt in 2004.

Based in Sydney, the practice deliberately pursues a range of project types from bespoke houses to housing prototypes, commercial and public commissions; operating in urban, suburban, rural and outback settings across Australia. Her practice's work has been recognised locally and internationally through publications, exhibitions and awards. These include the 2014 AIA Walter Burley Griffin Award, Sulman Medal and Lloyd Rees Award for the Prince Alfred Park and Pool Upgrade, and the 2016 Sulman Medal for the Kempsey Crescent Head Surf Life Saving Club. Awards are one thing, however, listening to Rachel, it is apparent her open-minded thinking and adventurous approach to design mean everything.

10 / 20

From a young age I was constantly making things. It was my play. Architecture seemed an almost natural progression, both measured and creative, and fundamentally broad, as if it were about the world!

From the ground up

I travelled with my family from age of 4.5 to 9. I was very fortunate—it was a childhood of adventure. As a child you really pick up on the sense of a place—its smell, its colour—a sense of its spatial density. You see and feel that places are different—the deep dark green of an English forest, the absence of trees in Norway, the dominance of the castle in Edinburgh, the coloured vaults and domes of Florence, the smell and labyrinthine quality of Fez, the grids and newness of Toronto. I think this fostered in me a genuine openness.

I grew up living in quite unusual homes—from an extended family setting with my grandparents, to a commune where my parents were two of 16 adults, to a VW Kombi, to a tiny four room house that had been carved out of a much bigger house, to a pair of tiny terraces again shared with my grandparents, and finally, at age 19, to a 1950s red brick bungalow. While none of them was architecturally designed, I was hard-wired for being open to 'possibility'.

My year 8 art teacher introduced me to architecture and from then on it became my focus. Oddly enough my father had wanted to be an architect but had to leave school early to help support his family. He never shared this passion until after I had committed to this career path. He didn't want to unduly influence me!

I was also drawn to architecture because it is part of something bigger—a city, a garden, a landscape. So I started on my architectural journey with my undergraduate degrees at the University of Sydney followed by a postgraduate Masters some years later in Barcelona.

Gender parity

I grew up in a gender-balanced home where both my parents worked and both were involved in raising their children. Then when I started architecture, there were more female students than male. What did become apparent however was the paucity of women in the faculty and as tutors. Particularly when you are in final year you are looking for professional role models. There were no female design tutors in my final year.

Today Parlour draws a researched focus on gender equity like never before in architecture anywhere! This is a vitally important first step to change. I hope it can reach the construction and development industries too, as we are so linked and impacted by attitudes there.

Starting in practice

The most important thing when I graduated was to be part of something really good. I didn't have a clear sense of where I wanted my future to lead me. Perhaps it was a combination of circumstance and inevitability that lead me to create my own practice with Nick Murcutt.

I worked for Hill Thalis in my early career and was one of their first employees. Philip Thalis had been a supervisor on my final year dissertation. It was an investigative study that looked at the influence of topography on the evolution and shape of Sydney, building on a mapping methodology that Philip had learned during his postgraduate study in Paris with Bruno Frontier. As teacher and student we shared a dogged enthusiasm for the city, for discovery and for precision. The opportunity to work with Philip—who was in a sense a mentor—was quite wonderful.

Hill Thalis had just been engaged to undertake an urban design study of Leichhardt. I was really drawn to this scale of thinking—it felt meaningful. At the same time I had started picking up small private residential jobs for family, extended family, and friends of family. Encouraged by my partner, Nick Murcutt, I took these on. I knew I would learn, through the doing, about materials, about construction, about the process of realising architecture. It would be years, decades before an urban design proposal was realised. Architecture was quicker! The opportunity to design space, make it, feel it, and reflect, was what the private projects offered me. And so from the beginning I worked for Hill Thalis part time, sub-letting studio space from Philip so that I could also work on my little projects.

Photography — Brett Boardman

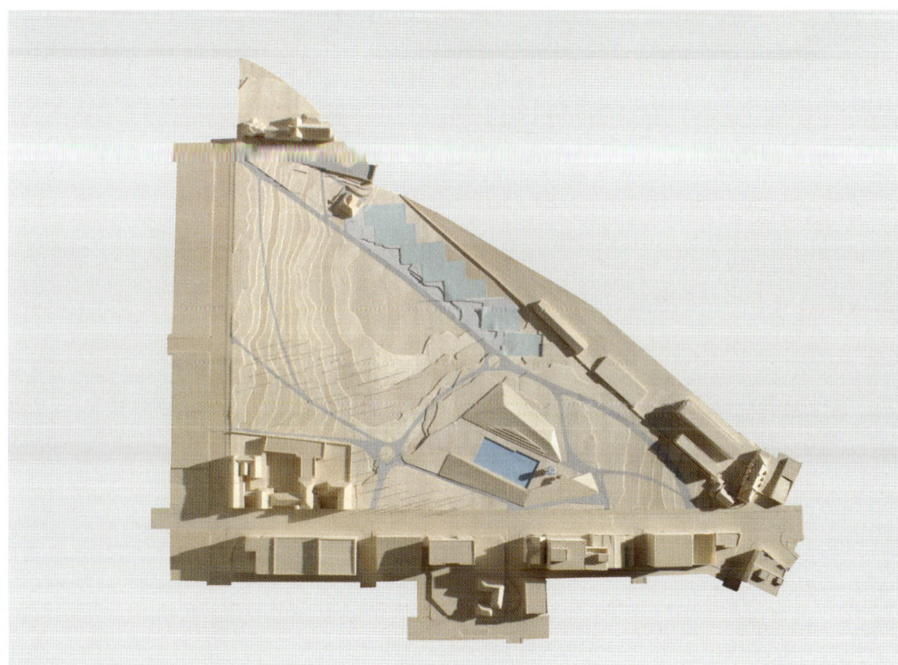

Prince Alfred Park + Pool Upgrade
Located at the edge of central Sydney, the project reinvigorates the under-ulitised 7.5ha park, and upgrades the tired public pool. The overriding principle was to promote landscape over built form, based on a conviction that in these inner urban areas green space is sacred. The old pool building was removed from the middle of the park, allowing the landscape to be visually opened. The new 1000m2 pool building is designed as a piece of 'folded landscape' with a green roof of native 'meadow' grasses that embeds it into the park.

From Dubai to Barcelona

I was working with friends at Randles Hill Straatveit on an urban project in Dubai when the events of September 11 took place.

1·5m

I relish diversity—there is nothing like a new problem to drive me. We have been fortunate in our small office to work on a wide range of project types. I hope that continues.

Needless to say, that project came to a halt within weeks. It felt like the right opportunity to pursue postgraduate study in architecture, something I had always wanted to do.

The following year I started a Masters in Barcelona, which ran over two half-year semesters. My teacher in Barcelona had worked with Álvaro Siza and was well acquainted with Rafael Moneo. He said that it was Moneo who inspired him as an architect. Siza was born an architectural genius but Moneo was a studied architect who demonstrated that through education one could learn to become exceptional. Apparently there isn't a book on architecture that Moneo hasn't read!

Nick looked after my private jobs whilst I was away. Nicholas Murcutt Architect had been established for some years and was developing an interesting portfolio of houses. When I returned from Barcelona, we joined our separate practices. It wasn't really planned but seemed somehow inevitable. We decided that together we would try to supplement our residential work by actively pursuing public projects, where our efforts would benefit a greater number of people, and where we could engage in city building in a different way to the single house. Within weeks we were lucky enough to be commissioned for the Shipwreck Lookout, a small public space within the Sydney Olympic Parklands.

Moments of consequence

Winning the Wilkinson for the Five Dock House was a wonderful shared experience for Nick and I. It was our first major award—a public validation of our joint creative process. Prince Alfred Park and Pool Upgrade is certainly our most significant achievement. It is a 7.5 hectare park at the edge of the city centre. The opportunity to reinvigorate a piece of city like that is what we aspire to—it is social sustainability. Recently, our practice

Photography — Brett Boardman

St Columba's Catholic Primary School
The site contains of a lineage of buildings dating back to 1901 —church, hall, presbytery, preschool and school. The project re-establishes a landscape curtilage as a way of integrating school church and hall, and the beautiful 'avenue' of trees along the street. The project is transformative. Discrete classrooms are replaced with open learning spaces that reflect new pedagogy.

completed a new entry to the Australian Museum. It is a small strategic project that has tremendous impact on the operation, public face, and engagement of the museum with its important immediate urban setting.

— *Has there been a moment when you felt the roof fell in?* Yes. Nick died while the Prince Alfred Park Pool was under construction. The build process for that job was difficult. It was our biggest commission at the time by far. I found the stress of that project, on top of the stress of losing your partner, extremely difficult to manage.

I realised that carrying stress over the weekend when you cannot do anything to relieve it is a complete waste of energy. It also makes it impossible to engage with small children at home in an effective or present sense.

I learnt to capture my stress in glass bottles on a Friday afternoon, put them on a shelf, and open them up again refreshed on a Monday morning. I also learnt the art of delegation!

— *What qualities do you look for when hiring for your practice?*
In a small practice the contribution of each individual is keenly felt. Everyone needs to be a good designer, everyone needs to be intelligent, everyone needs a good eye. I look for openness and I look for enthusiasm—someone who really wants to work in your practice, be part of your team.

Beautiful reward

Finding the way into a project—what shapes and defines it. This is the creative and intellectual challenge that I love. The evolution of a project happens over a long period, slowly coming to life as you move through the detail. Architecture is collaborative and the design process is like a long and focused conversation. I really enjoy these 'conversations' with inspired clients, with favourite engineers, with the architects and students in the office. After the project is built, I also particularly savour that moment when I forget myself as architect—picnicking with my children beside the slippery dip at Prince Alfred Park, sleepovers at the Castlecrag House, eating fishburgers with backs against the glazed brick walls at the surf club kiosk.

Collective ambition

Our office has shared studio space with landscape architect Sue Barnsley, and architects Joseph Grech and Durbach Block Jaggers, since forever! They are co-practitioners, collaborators, confidantes, critics, and friends. There is a collective ambition and a culture of high expectation. It is an environment where the making of architecture surrounds and is completely tangible—shelves laden with models, benches strewn with books, drawings, and ever-accumulating piles of samples.

Growing up my father had this saying 'if you are going to do a job do it properly or don't bother doing it at all!' Rather annoying as this may have been to a child, it somehow seeped into my being. Architecture requires such an effort by so many people over a sustained period of time, that you really want it all to be worth it!

Rising above commonplace

I relish diversity—there is nothing like a new problem to drive me. We have been fortunate in our small office to work on a wide range of project types. I hope that continues.

We are drawn to places that are distinctive, defined by their culture and how their culture has built and adapted to a particular topography and climate. We look to integrate every project with its setting in the broadest sense. It is a fundamental starting point. Sometimes this is about nature directly,

Life Lessons

10

Rachel Neeson

- Architecture essentially provides a platform for human activity
- Be open to every possibility
- Relish diversity
- Understand how places are different
- Embed sustainability within every design strategy
- Always consider architecture as being part of something bigger
- Architectural literacy is one of our most vital skills
- Architecture is collaborative, like a long and focused conversation

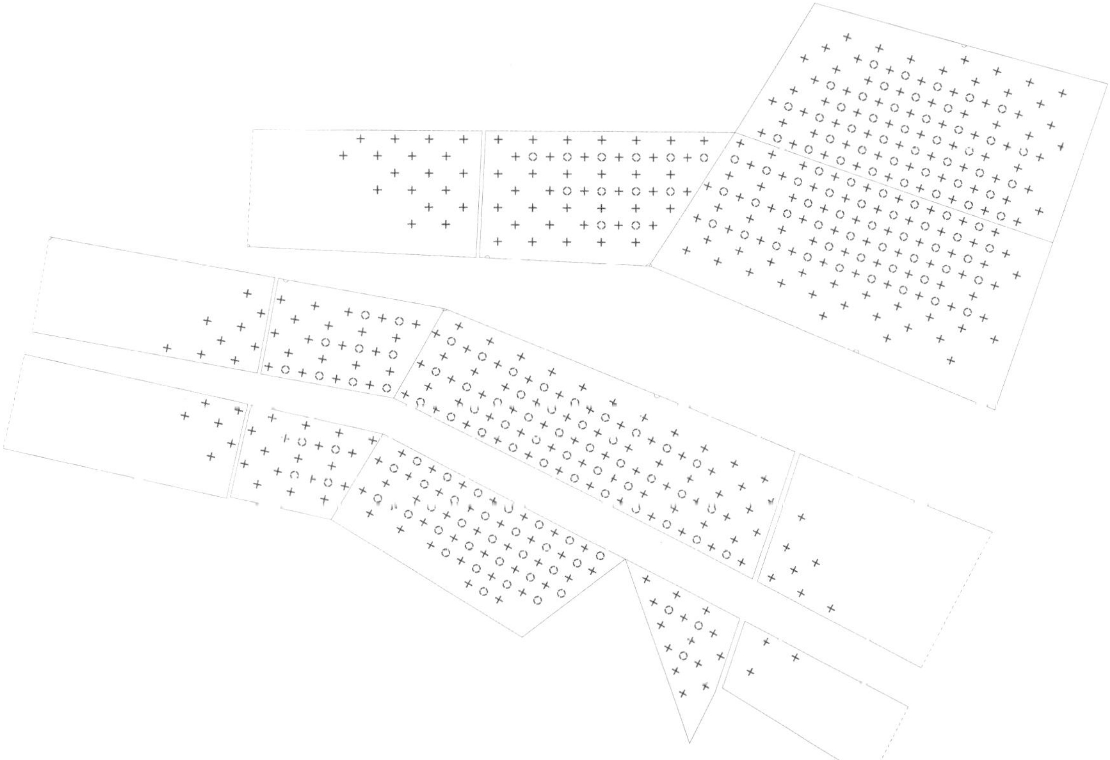

Architecture at its best delights the human spirit which makes all our lives better!

Photography — Brett Boardman

and sometimes it is more about an urban context or an historical continuity. The question of nature is inextricably linked to that of sustainability. We embed sustainability into our design strategies, minimising the operational energy in the buildings we create by using passive design to the greatest extent possible. This means engaging with orientation and climate.

Challenging preconceptions

Architecture essentially provides a platform for human activity. It was my late husband and co-founder of our practice, Nick, who taught me to challenge my own preconceptions about how people might use space—to think elementally about human occupation. He was a deeply intuitive person with great emotional intelligence. If the clients are avid readers, why not a house full of reading spots? If the clients love water gardens, why not a giant pond that fills the house and garden with the cooling sense of watery pond-life? If the clients are deeply attached to the old fireplace, why not keep it and shape a space around it that is small enough to really sense its warmth? As architects we constantly flicker between use, material and form, between inside and outside, between the pragmatic and the poetic.

That certain something

Sometimes it is something entirely outside of architecture that inspires. Inspiration for the Kempsey Crescent Head Surf Life Saving Club came out of a conversation with my partner, architect and surfer Stephen Neille. The idea surfaced after his comment that this building needed to be a 'beachy thing' to feel like it belongs at this beach. What is a 'beachy thing?' Something in the round, washed up by the sea? Something with a sense of leisure and play? My daughter's pipi shell collection inspired the material of the project—pipi shell coloured glazed bricks—and an unbuilt project by Diller and Scofidio, The Slow House.

— *Is the best education studying buildings rather than reading textbooks?* Architectural literacy—familiarity with architectural works—is one of the most important skills of an architect. Studying buildings is fundamental but this means understanding them holistically. The actual experience of them, but also where they sit in the culture of architecture, in a continuum of time. We need to read about them, as well as experience them and interrogate them through drawings.

— *Do works like the Beyoncé inspired building in Melbourne trivialise architecture?* The conflation of building and branding has proliferated ever since Gehry's Guggenheim Bilbao Museum. I understand this. Our pleated 'crystalline' entry facade at the Australian Museum was directly translated as the new museum logo! Quite possibly what this does is generate public discourse.

Our society is good at talking about our homes—it's where our personal wealth lies—but we are almost silent on the quality of every other building type. In Barcelona even the tabloid newspaper devotes four pages to architecture and urban issues every day. What this speaks of is a culture that values architecture and as a result, is demanding of it. This is very important.

Kempsey Crescent Head Surf Life Saving Club
Crescent Head is small beachside town and iconic surfing and fishing reserve. The new surf club replaces an existing building that was seriously dilapidated. In order to maintain the existing crown perpetual lease, the new building had to sit wholly within the footprint of the old, despite its awkward orientation and dimension. The building is designed in the round with a pitched roof and cut-away walls that produce a unique appearance on each side, reinforced by colour.

Photography — Brett Boardman

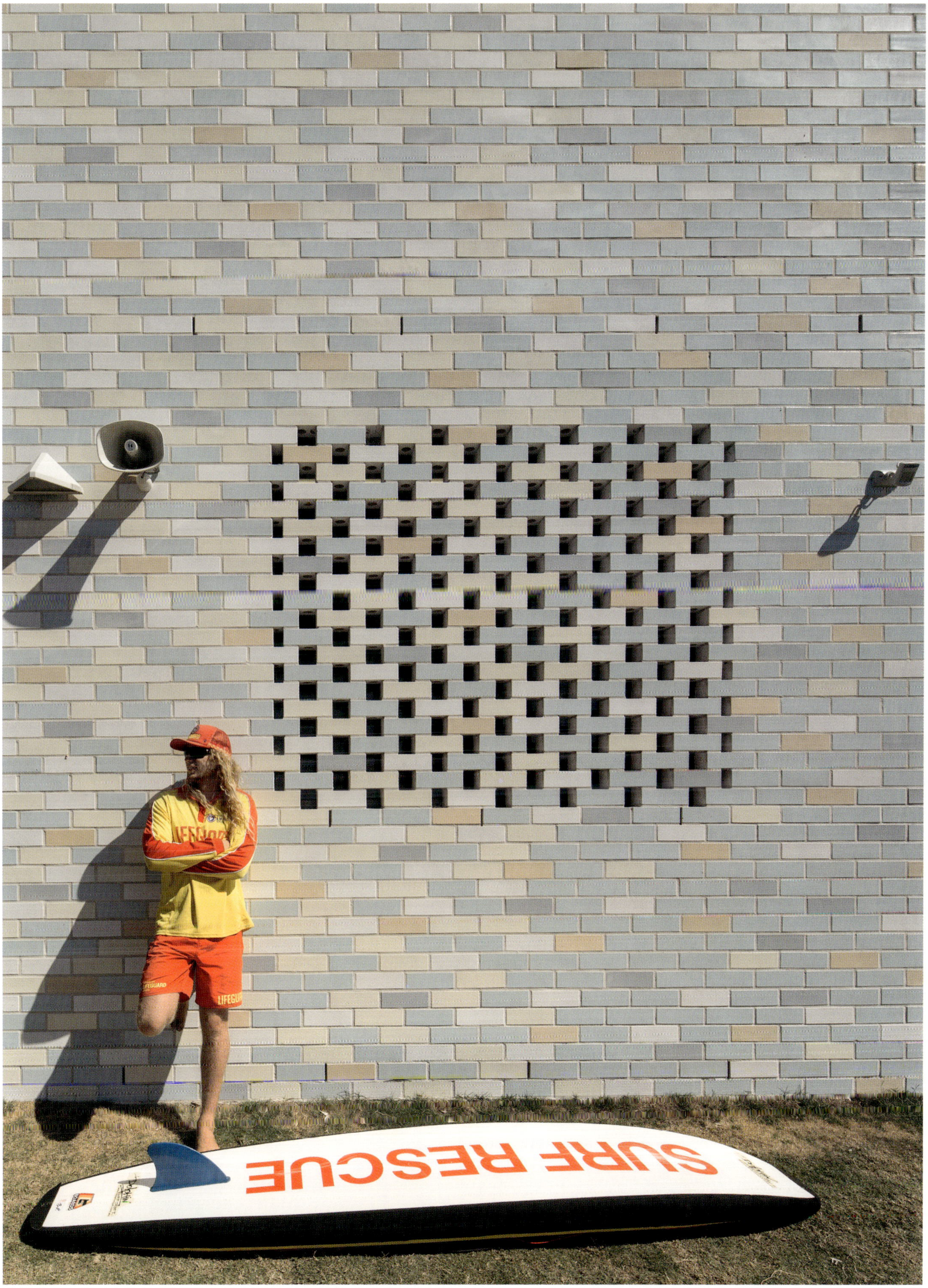

Photography — Brett Boardman

Sue Carr

Tactile tenacity

Sue Carr is the founder and principal director of Carr Design Group, a practice representing over forty years of work. Since co-founding the pioneering interior design firm Inarc, Sue's name has been synonymous with Australian design.

11 / 20

In a career that continues to push conventional boundaries, Sue's resolute commitment to the promotion of design in Australia has won her many awards—most notably her recognition as one of Australia's most influential women in The Australian Financial Review's Westpac '100 Women of Influence' award and in 2010—Australia's highest interior design accolade—the inaugural Interior Design Excellence Awards Gold Medal for Interior Design. Sue's work as a practitioner and indefatigable educator has been instrumental in redefining interior design; not simply as an afterthought but as a core discipline and vital component of architecture. She approaches every project with the belief that design has the power to make a positive difference to people's lives. Here Sue reveals the passion that drives her creativity from deep within.

University of Sydney Business School
The creation of a new type of university campus designed as a next generation learning and research environment fostering collaboration, creativity and the promotion of cutting edge business education. Indelibly linked by a striking circular timber clad staircase, a spectacular sculptural focal point to the main lobby reflects the movement of both people and ideas and a cohesive relationship between architecture and interior, form and function, public and private.

Architecture and design is imposed on us, in our daily lives, our homes and our places of work. Sometimes we vehemently oppose it and at other times we strongly support it, but either way it encourages us to think, debate and defend—actions that all contribute to the fabric of our lives.

Photography — Nichole England

Under the skin

I was immediately attracted to interior design because it was about the science of how we live and interact with one another in the environments that surround us. I was instantly captivated by the importance of blending the discipline of everyday living with the art of producing well-designed spaces. Design was original, different and new; it was a field full of possibilities and potential.

My interest has always been in looking to the future and our ability to predict and contribute to what it might hold; certainly this reveals the scientist in me. My interest in interiors was in understanding people's needs, how they live and work in a space, and developing detailed client briefs. I love this part of the process; the analysis of the brief is almost scientific, while the design is artistic.

I was not born into interior design and readily admit that it failed to hold any interest until I began university. On reflection, I realise that my entire childhood was geared towards a life in design; a life that would allow me to exercise my two greatest passions—science and art.

My mother had a strong artistic background and an involvement in fashion while my father was a chemist. At the time my parents strongly believed that a career in science was a more logical and professional path. Unlike Europe, or even the United States, Australia was yet to embrace the importance of design. There was little if any support for a creative culture that offered designers the opportunities to develop the industry to its full potential. As a result, I began studies in applied chemistry. Six months into the course, I had a sneaking suspicion that I had made a mistake.

Fledgling thinking

I enrolled at RMIT in the late 1960s and, at the time, interior design was a fledgling faculty so the subjects offered were experimental and varied. In philosophy we debated and analysed the works of Lewis Mumford; in Sociology we deliberated the impact of cities on their communities; and, in furniture construction we visited wood workshops to learn about form and shape.

I was passionate about the artistic subjects including pottery and painting. These subjects encouraged us to use our imagination and test the boundaries of our creativity and in so doing gave us a deeper and more enriched outlook on beauty. My background in science and mathematics also gave me an eye for detail and an ability to identify even the smallest discrepancies. Today I'm fascinated by subtlety in design. When you put all the subtleties together, the whole can be very strong.

— *Was it tougher for women back then or was it a non-issue?*

In regards to the field of design and architecture, I don't feel being a woman has been a disadvantage nor do I feel it has been an advantage. I'm just someone who has a passion for what they do. One of the difficulties I did find 'back then' was explaining the role of interior design to my clients. At the time many believed— maybe because I was female—that I was responsible for choosing the curtain and cushion fabrics. In meetings, they were seemingly unable to comprehend why an interior designer was involved before the building was even built. Many consider, even today, that interior design is an inferior discipline.

Starting in practice

Following graduation, I began working for a small architecture firm operated by my building construction lecturer. There were limited opportunities for interior designers so I was employed as an architect and trusted with a residential extension.

Starting my career with such a strong architectural focus has had a profound influence on the way I work. It taught me to understand the importance of space, form and light—all the tactile issues—the materiality, and subliminal parts; essentially thinking beyond the obvious or the superficial.

Following this invaluable experience, I moved to a larger practice in Collins Street, Melbourne. As is so often the case, the firm put political and commercial agendas well ahead of design merit and so I was exposed very early on to the age-old challenge of commerciality versus creativity.

A rock and a hard place

While I enjoyed working for the larger firm, I began to rock the boat and realised I had to take a leap of faith and begin my own practice. And so in 1971, together with a former colleague, I co-founded Inarc. We established our practice in a building in Murphy Street, South Yarra, which was home to an interesting mix of people and businesses. Merchant Builders, Henderson and Lodge, and renowned architects such as Kevin Borland were located in the same building. It was great to be working so closely with so many individuals of such varied disciplines and talents. Then the recession hit. One of our first major projects—a commercial fit out for Moule Hamilton and Derham (now Freehills)—was put on hold leaving us with no work to speak of. Through sheer tenacity and determination, we survived by designing beautiful homes for our close network of family and friends. Through word of mouth and on the back of many successful residential projects, the practice began to grow and become viable. By our fifth birthday, we had grown to a firm of ten people, and by our tenth we had grown to fifty.

Another reason for starting my own practice was my deep aversion to the aesthetic of the time. I was interested in hard floors, materiality and the cladding of forms. I was fascinated by the textural quality of the materials and how this could absorb and reflect light to produce its own aesthetic. Even then, I avoided working with strong colours and patterns, opting for a palette.

Beautiful reward

The opportunities presented to us as interior designers and architects are infinite. People will always require spaces to inhabit, and as interior designers we have the unique opportunity and inevitable responsibility of defining those spaces. The future will see designers called upon to have more technical knowledge in specialised areas. There will be an increasing demand to possess strong skills to work as a team, work more closely with related professions and accept greater responsibility for the protection of the natural environment.

South Yarra Residence
Built in the 1920s the property began life as a pair of duplexes. The completed project restores and celebrates the beauty and historical significance of the original built form juxtaposed against the crisp detailing of a timeless, contemporary addition.
Photography — Derek Swalwell

We have to champion quality over trends. We have to stop chasing the new, because far too often this has resulted in only the arbitrariness of fad.

Courtyard House (Left)
Modern without overt references, the design embraces shadow and light. A refined palette of materials—cement rendered walls, honed concrete, steel, aluminium, glass—allude to a simplicity of form and function reminiscent of houses built in the 60's and create a compelling rhythm of opposites: solidity and transparency, light and dark, cool and warm, hard and soft.

Frame House (Right)
Situated on a large block in Melbourne's inner east, this family property exposes little to the street. However, concealed behind the textured stucco wall, a striking house is revealed within a lush secret garden. The rhythm of the colonnade and overall proportions evoke the elegance of Japanese architecture. The house is bold and contemporary with a robust steel frame supporting a finely detailed metal screen and zinc cladding.

Photography — John Gollings

Photography — Gorta Yuuki

There is nothing quite like visiting a building site and being able to experience a space that you had only ever conceived in your mind. After all the drawings, the meetings, the plans, and the scrutinising of the tiniest details, turning your vision into bricks and mortar is incredibly rewarding.

All these years later I am still full of anticipation and wonder at all the parts of a project—from the first muddy excavation of the site to the fine detailing of a staircase.

I enjoy the experience of being on site. It is such a collaborative process and takes a completely different set of skills to be able to work collectively with the project team. In your studio you are in control; it's your team, your tools and your experience. On site, however, there are so many variables and so many challenges that it becomes a concerted team effort to ensure the delivery of the vision.

As I've gained more experience, I've learnt to successfully work alongside some of the very best contractors. This makes the process a little less stressful, as the margin for error is greatly reduced.

Progressing the profession

The rush for development is compromising the credibility of design, and perhaps nowhere more than in Melbourne and Sydney. As is too often the case, developers will employ brilliant architects to design beautiful buildings. As soon as the planning permit is approved, contracts are reneged and less experienced architectural firms are recruited to complete the project. Sadly so much original thought and design intent is lost in the transition.

The same applies to interiors. I am increasingly frustrated by developments that encompass great architecture but mediocre interiors. My frustrations in this area—and my belief that the two disciplines are infallibly linked—led me to establish Carr Architecture. This has meant creating a complete design service, where our strength lies equally across both fields as opposed to interior design being seen as the 'poor cousin'.

Thankfully as a nation, who didn't recognise the term 'interior design' less than fifty years ago, we have come a long way. However, there is always need for improvement and never a moment for complacency. There will always be the challenge for a greater level of understanding and an increased willingness to accept the value of good design (inside and out) so that in the future it becomes part of our national psyche such as that which is so evident in Scandinavia, Italy and France.

Today there is a new architectural and design ambition to not just enhance the urban environment but also to respect the global landscape. Neither architects nor anyone who is concerned about the future can disregard the effects of climate change, the widening gulf between the rich and poor; the instability of our social infrastructure; and, the ongoing threat of war and displacement.

Life Lessons

11

Sue Carr

- Think beyond the obvious or superficial
- Champion timeless design over fad
- Embrace technology but never forget the beauty of tactile, timeless design
- Lead through collaboration
- Appreciate the way light plays on materials
- Design with confidence from a place of pride, passion and humility
- Understand that with every opportunity comes great social responsibility
- Realise the difference between the scientific nature of the brief and the artistic quality of the design response

Australia Post
The rebranding of Australia Post's business model is explicitly woven throughout the design, recasting itself for the new digital age. This comes across in the choice of materiality, lighting and symbolism. Nowhere is this more clearly evident than in the polished mirrored-and-marbled foyer, where a nineteenth-century red pillar post box provides an endearing nod to the past. An air of sophisticated formality abounds, achieved through the use of sharp detailing, high-end finishes and elegant furnishings.
Photography — Earl Carter

Frank Lloyd Wright said, 'architects should always design from the inside out.' I don't entirely agree with this statement, the practice of design is much more complex, layered and elastic.

We live in tumultuous and unsettling times, but breakthroughs in technology, materiality and communications have enabled us to discover and share the tools that will advance humanity on a global scale.

Rising above commonplace

We need to keep driving and educating our graduates. They are fortunate to be working in this climate of great change and an environment that challenges the presuppositions of the past century.

The quality of university design degrees has grown from strength to strength. They continue to arm graduates with a strong and dedicated focus on the foundation elements of design; a platform from which they can create distinct, responsive, and dynamic environments. The fresh outlook and intelligence that new graduates bring to our practice is considerable. I love watching as ideas go from the page to life as they sketch, model, sculpt, and digitise.

— *What advice would you give a student when they hit a brick wall?* I would advise of the need for them to have a strong belief in themselves and to be confident in their design thinking and vision. They need to possess a sense of pride and passion but also humility. The only way students and young graduates can develop and grow is by listening to people with experience. By absorbing knowledge, students can gain a deeper understanding of the brief, the client, the challenge, and importantly a solution that breaks through the barrier.

Designers and architects need to listen to their intuition, their emotional response, their gut feeling. When you successfully combine this instinctiveness with the external factors of people, places, environments and experiences, the right design response will present itself.

I am constantly seeking ground breaking ideas and concepts. I am continually motivated and influenced by the related fields of design, fine arts, the social and behavioural sciences, technology, travel and the unique Australian environment.

I am inspired by travel on an annual basis to a place I have not been before. I am passionate about cities. They represent the heart of a culture and the spirit of a country. I enjoy losing myself in a beautiful city: exploring its rivers, its narrow laneways, its tallest skyscrapers, and its wide boulevards - the excitement of stumbling across unforgettable underground galleries, inconspicuous restaurants, hidden theatres, and secret retail destinations. I enjoy stopping in a café and simply observing the richness of a city through its people—their style, cultural diversity, conversations, language, way of life and the way they are a reflection of a city that is theirs.

— *What qualities do you look for when hiring for your practice?* I always favour candidates who are authentic and genuine; people who know themselves and are not afraid to show who they are. I also value designers who are not afraid to challenge the status quo; bringing new problem solving ideas into use. This often flourishes in egalitarian cultures such as ours.

Radical transformation

In over forty years of business, I have experienced many challenges none more so than often being encouraged to design interiors that would appeal to the 'fashion at the time'. But it is through my belief that good design has the power to make a positive difference, that I have continued to rebel against fads and trends. Every project presents a new client, a new opportunity, a new location, a new time in life. In response to this we are always examining and learning different and exciting new ways of doing things and applying this knowledge to our projects.

Undoubtedly the biggest change has been today's fast-paced global environment and the way we as designers have had to harness the power of digital technology to stay competitive.

Since the beginning, technology has played a crucial role in our business. A decade ago while travelling I met with several European designers and learnt about their innovative approach to three-dimensional design technology. The possibilities of this technology were endless however the risks were great as its introduction involved extensive retraining of the entire team. As one of the first design practices to introduce Autodesk Revit in Australia the risks inevitably were worth it. Revit enables us to produce ideas and design concepts efficiently, quickly and in greater detail so that a client can understand the space at a very early stage.

The late architect, Philip Johnson, once stated that 'great technologies breed great architecture'. Technology is not a limitation but an extraordinary opportunity. I continue to be excited by the infinite possibilities it presents. Using robots, we can erect structures economically and in half the time of more traditional construction methods. This allows us to explore and investigate new aesthetics and ideas that otherwise would have been too costly.

Norton Rose Fulbright National Branding
The design infuses architectural detailing with three-dimensional spatial branding to create a fit out that is inventive and highly visual. The use of graphic patterns in unexpected ways creates a distinctive, modernist visual language providing a striking and professional introduction to the firm whilst referencing the iconic elements of each city's locale.

Despite the drastic changes in technology, the fundamentals of our practice remain constant; an understanding of construction, an appreciation for the quality of materials, and the beauty of clever, timeless design.

Photography — Ian ten Seldam

As technology continues to develop and evolve, we are exposed to the possibility of realising forms and designs on a much larger and more complex scale.

Look at the work of Frank Gehry for example. In the 1990s, Gehry pioneered digital design in architecture by using CATIA software to elevate designs and translate them directly into a process of fabrication and construction. He was able to realise concepts he never even dreamed were possible. Further, UK architect Amanda Levete uses modern materials and technology to create shelter, expressing this in beautiful and profound ways.

The only drawback with technology is that it can encourage a 'cut and paste' mentality leading to mediocre work. Today, it's easy to reference what has been created before. This can lead to designs lacking in original thought.

Passion within

I feel that finally the tide is turning and we are becoming more aware of the value of design—the importance of design in the creation of home as sanctuary, in the productivity of a workspace, in the hotel guest experience.

Despite the drastic changes in technology, the fundamentals of our practice remain constant: an understanding of construction; an appreciation for the quality of materials; and, the beauty of clever, timeless design.

Photography — James Braund

Photography — James Braund

Melissa Bright

Pragmatic poetry

Melissa Bright is the owner and founding director of MAKE architecture—an emerging practice that has already gathered a collection of built work that displays a striking conversation with Melbourne architectural heritage. With Its work predominantly in residential building—alterations and addition—the careful understanding of occupational use is complemented by an intrinsic interest in material specificity.

12 / 20

MAKE thoughtfully approaches projects with the ambition that they do more, offer more; for the client, the neighbourhood and the broader site context. This reflects Mel's belief that every project is a privilege and opportunity to contribute positively to the fabric of its place. Believers in quality not quantity, MAKE looks for delight and efficiencies in design and focuses on ways buildings can make our lives better. In this interview the quality of Mel's deep design thinking certainly shines through.

Local House, St Kilda, Melbourne
This project has been designed to be robust and durable; to take the knocks of family life. Whilst it's not precious or delicate, it didn't mean that ideas of beauty and delight weren't important to the design thinking.

I felt like there was more opportunity to make a difference in architecture. That it is less about fashion and style than other design professions. Architecture has an ability to make a contribution to our cities and the way people live. On one end of the scale you need to keep the rain out, at the other we want to create something that gives delight—light, space and poetry.

Photography — Sam Wong

Photography — Peter Bennetts

From the ground up

I loved art and design in high school and at the last minute I changed my university preferences from engineering to architecture. I realised that with architecture I could combine both the rational and the creative.

Even at university I still wasn't sure and I was initially a pretty average student. I studied at RMIT, and at the time it felt like a very overwhelming place. I was straight out of high school and often felt out of my depth. Design studios during first year were run as vertical studios, so I was in classes with students that had already been there for three years. Many were mature age students, some who had been trying to get into the degree for many years, they were really focused and happy to be there. The quality of work they did was amazing. For a long time I stayed quiet—too unsure to say much at university. I took a long time to build confidence and find my voice. I learnt that good design is about perseverance and testing, more about hard work than anything else—1% inspiration 99% perspiration. Things started to click and architecture slowly got under my skin. By the end of the degree I was very committed and determined to do well. Now I can't quite imagine doing anything else.

My family are all quite rational with an engineering background. I was brought up with a strong work ethic and a great sense that integrity is important in a person. This has shaped my approach to things and how I run the business. I still often talk with my dad for advice on how to deal with certain issues; his support has always been amazing to have in the background. I also love that practising as an architect requires pretty diverse and varied set of skills from so many disciplines. It is constantly challenging and I feel like I am learning all the time.

Starting in practice

I enjoyed working in larger practices prior to starting MAKE. However, the idea of exploring my own design ambitions and being the master of my own destiny was increasingly attractive.

Initially in many ways I thought of it as a way to have more flexibility and control in my life. I wanted to have children and liked that I could choose my own hours and work load. I also loved that in a small practice you switch from all aspects—design, practice management, site visits, talks, waterproofing details.

In the early years, I took on any job and tried to make the most out of it. The first projects were very small, bathroom and kitchen renovations for friends of friends. Each project has led to the next and they have slowly improved along the way. In a large practice on bigger projects it is easier to get pigeonholed.

Photography — Sean Fennessy

The idea that there is a 'light bulb' moment of inspiration is not a true reflection of how we design. Good architecture has so many layers. You can't solve that in an instant. Hard work and research might get you there though.

With each project taking two to three years we are really only in our third round of projects. I think we should talk about architecture years like dog years where three years equates to one year. Making it happen is a lot about perseverance.

— *Has there been a moment when you felt as if the roof fell in?* I don't think there was an actual moment where I felt like the roof caved in, but there have been many obstacles and difficulties. In the earlier years of practice I found any difficult issue quite stressful, I would lay awake at night worrying. I think that has been something that I have learnt to get better at managing. Experience has taught me to take a deep breath and understand that issues are normal and that they just need to be calmly worked through with those involved. With most issues the best way forward is good clear communication and I would always tackle any problem head on rather than avoid the situation. I think that even in difficult situations you can maintain integrity. Empathy is also important remembering that everyone has their own concerns and worries.

Beautiful reward

I'd like to be able to say that running my own practice has given me great flexibility with family and kids. The reality in recent times is that I am working really hard and I don't see the kids as much as I would like.

Practising as an architect though gives me great joy and satisfaction through making something. I love that my job most often doesn't feel like work, I look forward to being there and I'm always excited to see our designs come to life.

Seeing something built is still the greatest reward for what we do. This is highly motivating. Those moments when you are sure you did the right thing and the built reality is right.

Progressing the profession

There is much conversation about architects becoming irrelevant. Conversely I think that as the pressure increases to densify our cities architects have an important role to play.

To allow for population growth and stop further sprawl our suburbs must increase in density. The current model of oversized houses located increasingly greater distances from employment has meant a huge reliance on cars that is unsustainable.

Current standards of buildings especially in the Melbourne apartment arena are not good enough. Apartments are built for selling, not for making the homes for residents of our cities in the future. The real estate agent is king and the conversation is so much about what is known to sell. There is no room for innovation or something that hasn't been seen before because it hasn't been tested in the market. If we are to live more closely to one another, good innovative design is essential to ensure the living quality is not reduced. Architecture, with the support from planning, can provide a socially sustainable built environment that encourages connections to communities.

Rising above commonplace

— *Do you think the present education system really measures up?* I am really impressed with some of the graduates coming out of university. They are so skilled, ambitious and organised. I don't remember being like that. Many people complain about graduates not being technically skilled enough. However, I think one of the most important things an architecture degree teaches is design thinking. If you can learn this then it can be applied to any problem. Balancing a degree with working part-time in practice is an essential thing. The realities of practising as an architect can really only be learnt on the job.

— *What advice would give a student when they hit a brick wall?* Go around it. Brick walls in design can only be escaped by doing more work, tackle the problem from a different direction. The worst thing a student can do when they come to a design roadblock is to stare at a white sheet of paper. Test something, test anything, whatever you do don't do nothing. The reality is design can be really hard and sometimes it feels like you won't crack a project. One of the questions we ask in the studio during the design stage is, 'are you excited about seeing it on site?' If the answer isn't 'yes' then the design isn't good enough yet.

In terms of career and life, a good friend once said to me that he had, 'decided to start walking through the open doors and that he was going to stop banging his head against the closed ones.' This has stayed with me. I like the idea that one should just work hard and keep an eye out for opportunities. See the opportunities that are presented and grab them with both hands.

— *What qualities do you look for when hiring for your practice?* MAKE is like a little family so it is hugely important to find the right people. Durable designers that can handle robust design discussions are essential. We all like to stand around and debate design, so egos need to be left at the door.

THE RETURN OF THE KING
THE TWO TOWERS

Life Lessons

12

Melissa Bright

- Balancing a degree with working part-time in practice is essential
- Design isn't a commodity, it belongs to the community
- Aim to delight through design efficiency and social sustainability
- Great architectural design has so many layers. It can't simply be solved in a light bulb moment
- When you hit a brick wall test something, test anything. Whatever you do, don't do nothing
- Taking a deep breath can get you a long way in life
- There are so many times a project can be pushed off the rails. Push it at every stage, don't give up
- Great design is like a future gift to ourselves and our clients

Photography — Peter Bennetts

The best people are just trying to work towards finding the right design solution and it gets done as a team in a collaborative manner. It doesn't matter who did it but that we got to the right answer.

— *Is there a common DNA running through architects?* Everyone is different and there are so many ways to practise architecture. However, I do think that to be a successful architect you have to be really persistent and determined. There are so many times that one thing or another can threaten a good outcome for a project. You just have to persevere, keep pushing and keep inventing new solutions. Being an agile problem solver is also handy, as so many factors have to be considered all at once. Constraints of budget, client, constraints of building, all make it hard to produce good design.

Thinking through breakthoughs

I don't know if we have breakthroughs—more things that we test and obsess over that slowly come into focus. It is often an accumulation of ideas that sit in the background. After a while I see repeated things in our work that make sense to me.

The right outcome is such a layered solution. It must do many things, so this never really comes as a breakthrough, more as a series of things that finally come together. There is always compromise and I focus on the one bit that is not perfect. Always feeling slightly worried or dissatisfied—this certainly drives me.

The idea that there is a 'light bulb' moment of inspiration is not a true reflection of how we design. Good architecture has so many layers. You can't solve that in an instant. Hard work and research might get you there though.

Architecture can transform our cities and suburbs and affect the way we live and interact with each other. We have the ability to create cities for people and communities. Embracing this positive ethos contributes to a socially sustainable community; knowing that this will ultimately help a suburb to be a happy place to live.

Ultimately I think good design is like a future gift to ourselves, and our clients. This is what really drives me—architecture is hard so it might as well be good.

Myrtle Tree House
This extension to an existing Californian Bungalow continues MAKE architecture's careful explorations with inventive but modest architecture that engages carefully with context and site conditions. The aim was to keep as much of the existing building as possible, and to carefully and poetically stitch the new work into the fabric of the original.

Lisa-Maree Carrigan

Holistic intimacy

Lisa-Maree studied architecture and graduated from the University of Newcastle with First Class Honours in 1992, and then went on to work in large practices in Sydney and London. She returned to Sydney in 2001 and joined GroupGSA, where she has been a director for the last decade.

Lisa-Maree's ability to think laterally, while maintaining a strong project direction, has won her numerous awards for design and master planning. She has worked on projects in over twelve countries including Australia, UK, across Europe, Asia and the Middle East. Lisa-Maree has a passion for holistic design, from the macro-scale urban design to the finer detail of furniture and artwork. She loves working collaboratively with clients and leading teams to design innovative living environments. In this engaging chapter we get up close and personal with Lisa-Maree as she shares the holistic thrill of it all.

13 / 20

I decided to become an architect at age nine. Given my upbringing, it seemed like a completely logical and natural choice. It was a choice that I never waivered from, even when I was in high school. I honestly can't imagine doing anything else.

Domain
The Dominion residential development located on the heritage site of Caritas on Forbes Street, Darlinghurst contains 110 residential apartments, commercial areas and 142 car parking spaces. The materials palette of the buildings focuses on rich, natural materials of sandstone, glass, zinc and timber. Operable louvre and facade shading systems provide maximum flexibility to the residents and a benchmark sustainable response.

Concrete perfume

I was surrounded by construction and property from an early age. I suppose you could say a large component of the lure to architecture was environmental. My father is a developer. Prior to being in development, he had a construction company building water treatment plants, water towers and other infrastructure projects. So site sheds, remote locations, and large machinery were all very familiar to me as a young child. When his focus switched to development the nature of the work changed, and it became more interesting to me—built form in the city. The process of creating and building places for people to live in resonated. From the age of nine I knew I wanted to be an architect. I was always art focused and worked on creative projects at home. There was a confluence between nature and nurture that made architecture seem completely logical as a choice. As a child, the drive for development also meant that we were in a frequent state of renovation and moving, doing one place up and then selling it and moving somewhere new. Over time this crystallised in my mind two things: firstly, I wanted to be part of the design and creative process, not a developer; secondly, I didn't want to live in a state of perpetual change. The other interesting aspect of growing up in my younger to mid-teen years, in a household focused on development and property, I was exposed to the strong work ethic that was required. Work permeated all aspects of home life, with even holidays interjected with development opportunities, site searches and unexpected visits to other's building sites. The positive side of this was the real life example I had of the importance of choosing a career that you were passionate about.

Having been exposed to heavy construction engineering, architecture and interior design from a young age, I could see the choices but I was always drawn to architecture the most. Initially it was the scale of the work, with a focus on form and context, the shaping of the built environment that held my interest. Over time this extended from the macro-scale urban design and architecture to a discovery of love of the other end of the spectrum—the micro-scale detail junctions and materials, and the layering and finish that is more interior focused. It has been an interesting journey that

Photography — Tyrone Branigan

has taught me that I am happiest when designing and considering both scales of a project. When I started to work on hotel projects, I found great alignment with the focus on macro and micro, and they are still the project type I enjoy the most.

New thinking

I studied architecture at the University of Newcastle, where the course was run as problem-based learning. I enjoyed the course tremendously and believe that the problem-based curriculum worked well for me. It closely aligned with real practice; researching and learning directed towards a specific project typology design challenge rather than separate streamed subjects. The year coordinators typically were good mentors, although there isn't any one in particular that stood out. The architectural course at the time was five days-a-week, with mostly full days at university, and for the final year long hours working in the studio. A lot of influence came from fellow students as we would critique each other's work and help each other. We also had a very competitive and high achieving year, so we pushed each other more than the tutors did. The importance of consistent work, the importance of being able to present your ideas, and the importance of having a strong concept basis for design are the key learnings I recall from my studies.

In architecture, making sure that you have a coherent and defensible conceptual basis upon which to found the design response is very important.

This became evident when presenting to critique sessions at university. One of the great training aspects of studying architecture was the regular process of having to stand up in front of all of your peers and a jury to present your scheme and respond to challenges. The robust nature of this was a great basis for professional life, where presenting and communicating ideas is a critical skill. I feel fortunate to have studied there at that time, and have maintained a connection to the university as a Faculty Board Advisor for the last eight years.

— *Was it tougher for women back then or was it a non-issue?* When I started studying there was a 50/50 split between men and women and I perceived it as a complete non-issue. By the time final year came around, we were a class of less than half the size of the starting year. The gender split in the final year was more like 30/70.

Starting in practice

My first job post-graduation in professional practice was during the recession in the early 1990s. I was very fortunate to have previously worked for a small office during my year out between degrees, doing residential projects for architect John McKinney, who used to work in the Government Architect's office with Andrew Andersons. The recommendation from John got me an interview with Andrew at PTW Architects, and a job offer during the recession. Andrew was a mentor to me. I learnt a tremendous amount from him while at PTW and was very lucky to be given some great opportunities and projects to work on. Then when I moved to a larger practice I really enjoyed the scale change and the diversity. It's this attraction of the larger scale projects that has kept me in large practice; as well as the ability to change typology focus and also work overseas.

Photography – Tyrone Branigan

Kingston Foreshore
The project develops an urban residential environment organised around a series of public domain spaces, with an integrated landscape and public art concept by Indigo Kleinert fronting Wentworth Avenue designed to be viewed from the car.

My husband is an architect working in large practice and we are frequently asked why we never chose to have a practice together. We met working together, so it's never been a question of professional synergy. Rather that we both enjoy large scale projects, the sort that are not given to small practices. It is also significantly easier to take a substantial holiday together without it impacting the practice. A great benefit of having colleagues and partners who can be there when you are not. Beyond the project scale and type diversity, I prefer being able to focus on the type of work I enjoy doing, with the support of larger practice infrastructure for the tasks that I don't enjoy so much. Working in larger practice has also afforded me the ability to travel for work to some great places, and to gain experiences I am grateful for.

Life and design balance

The balance is challenging and constantly changing for me. Having a partner who is in the same profession is incredibly helpful in that he understands the demands and requirements of both the profession and the role. A shared passion for architecture and design makes it much easier when you travel. There's no frustration with going off to see another building or finding that your several thousand photos of holidays are 90% of buildings without people. The balancing of the demanding role has meant sacrifices, but typically that's been sleep rather than family life. Being available or 'on' all the time allows you the flexibility to go to school concerts and the like. However the work doesn't go away, it needs to get done. What 'balance' means for everybody is different. The essential thing I have found is to understand what it means for me personally. Understanding your own threshold for stress and what tools or circumstances make it easier to deal with the demands of the profession are also critical. For instance, I prefer to be contactable even when on holiday, so that I know what's going on, and if there's a problem I can help address it or fix it before it gets out of hand. The peace of mind I get from that allows me to enjoy myself more than the worry that I get from not knowing.

Life Lessons

13

Lisa - Maree Carrigan

- Be proactive and generously collaborative
- If the diagram isn't right the building won't be
- Communicating ideas well is a critical skill
- Holistic approaches produce the best design outcomes
- Micro makes the macro sing
- Lateral thinking is essential
- Understand your strengths, weaknesses and stress threshold
- Robust scrutiny steels you for future challenges
- Appreciating typology is key to design originality

Sydney Central Student Accommodation
The brick facades reference the adjacent brick heritage Briston building and are highly articulated to provide depth and diversity within the architectural expression.
Photography — Tyrone Branigan

A shared passion for architecture and design makes it much easier when you travel. There's no frustration with going off to see another building, or finding that your several thousand photos of holidays are 90% of buildings without people.

Beautiful reward

It's a fantastic feeling to have a creative response that resonates with the challenge posed—be it built form or any other area of design. You feel a certainty and a real adrenalin rush when you have that moment of creative energy based on a solid analysis or response. The two go hand-in-hand, for a meaningful design you need the blend of the quantitative with the qualitative. The pleasure that comes from that creative moment, the genesis of a much longer design journey of iterations and development—both fulfilling and addictive.

It's also memorable for each project; for every project I have worked on in over twenty years of practice, I know what the creative moment was. That level of involvement in a project's DNA is what I find professionally rewarding. What I enjoy seeing realised is the built outcome. There is always a journey of project development through the gestation of a project, but the original concept or idea—the creative genesis—should be visible.

Progressing the profession

There are many challenges to the credibility of architects, the development process being only one of those. The nature of development heightens the economic imperatives. It's the degree to which it dominates that differs from client to client, although the core fundamentals remain. Development is essential to growth in our cities, it's a reality. With the Public Private Partnership method becoming the norm for more capital-heavy projects, development processes are now becoming embedded drivers in project typologies that have historically been publicly funded. The challenge as architects is to actively understand these commercial drivers so that we can better work with them to ensure meaningful urban outcomes. The balance and tension is between the economic understanding and the qualitative drivers; when, as architects, we are striving to ensure the built form makes a positive contribution and is the best it can be. While development is building now, the predominance of it as a delivery method now could mean that the economic overlay drives the outcome away from the memorable and outstanding to the middle ground of the well-executed norm.

Rising above commonplace

For me the holistic approach to design produces the best design outcome. The cohesion and conceptual clarity is evident and compelling when this is the case.

— *What qualities do you look for when hiring for your practice?* Attitude foremost, then talent. A proactive person with a collaborative approach and raw talent I would hire immediately as you can teach skill and finesse approach, but the essential nature and disposition of someone is incredibly important when you are adding a new team member. This of course can vary depending upon the role, so beyond the appropriateness of talent, skill and experience for a specific role, a collaborative and open approach is really important. Without a good 'cultural fit', the right skill set won't work out for the team or practice as a whole.

— *Is there a common DNA running through successful architects?* A passion for design and lateral thinking are essential to being successful in design outcomes. Resilience and perseverance are also very important characteristics to carry you through the project journey. The best architects are also those who don't see the boundaries in disciplines, where the thinking starts at the macro or urban level, carries through the built form and extends to the interior detail, textures, way finding and artwork.

Radical transformation

We are at an interesting point in the profession. I see completely different focuses with younger architects in their work. There are those whose focus is predominantly on the doing in terms of parametric modelling and software—where the tangible architecture is almost an abstract concept. There is some extremely interesting work and exploration that comes from this, but the reality of creating spaces for people is secondary to the digital and technical challenge. Then there are those who conversely seek out opportunities to work on real projects on site, and to do project typologies that can make an impact on the quality of peoples' lives. Outside of mainstream work, but within the industry, there are the many volunteering opportunities. These include working with overseas aid, Habitat for Humanity and locally PIF which more and more younger architects are becoming involved with, irrespective of the focus within their professional lives. This has certainly escalated since I was a younger architect. I do see more focus going towards creating meaningful contributions to the built environment and humanity, which is greatly encouraging.

Hilton Fiji
GroupGSA re-visioned and re-planned an existing master plan for the site in order to create a resort concept of individual villa buildings set in a lush garden and water court landscape. The master plan focuses on concentrating the villa footprints on a tight site 1.5 kilometres long, creating open space and a rich guest experience.

Clare Cousins

Relationships forged

Clare Cousins studied architecture at RMIT and took a semester at the TU in Berlin. Since establishing Clare Cousins Architects in 2005, the practice has grown organically and works across diverse cultural and commercial projects. Clare Cousins Architects are specialists in small to large scale residential projects.

14 / 20

Whatever the typology or scale, each of Clare's projects evokes a domestic quality, celebrating the experience of space and life within it. With many repeat clients, Clare values the process of architecture and construction, and the relationships forged. A recipient of the Australian Institute of Architects (AIA) National Emerging Architect Prize, Clare is actively involved in the broader design community and was recently elected to the National Council of the Australian Institute of Architects. Clare advocates the many benefits of architecture to ensure that good design is valued in society. An inaugural investor in Nightingale 1.0, Clare supports the landmark triple bottom line development model for its social and sustainable benefits for the community and is now undertaking her own Nightingale project. This chapter is essential reading if you're curious about creativity that forges relationships to enrich the spaces that shape our lives.

Baffle House
This contemporary garden pavilion is a compact addition to an Edwardian cottage. Conceived to maximise exposure to a small, sculptural garden, it achieves porosity between the interior and exterior. Smaller projects are an opportunity to test ideas, especially when courageous clients are willing to take measured risks.

Architecture combines the creative arts with science and logic, which is the perfect balance for me.

From the ground up

Architecture was not a childhood dream; rather I stumbled across it as a university preference over studying engineering. In many ways they both demand an understanding of form, materials, textures and an astute creative eye.

I think that the emotive qualities of architecture can have lasting memories. As a child my family was fortunate to live in a number of different countries, and our regular visits to different cultural buildings and the theatre have really stayed with me. I have especially strong childhood memories of the colours and material textures of The Barbican in London.

During high school I had various creative pursuits. I played the piano, was involved in drama and school musicals, and I enjoyed sewing and altering op-shop purchases. Initially, I was nervous that I wasn't creative enough to study architecture. Fortunately, there was no folio requirement the year I applied; entry was based on school results and an interview. RMIT was not my first choice, as a 17 year old the university campus influenced my decision over the course content and RMIT's architecture department was in the midst of construction. As it turned out, RMIT was the right university for me. It took a few semesters, but they taught me to think more conceptually and less pragmatically, which I needed.

I learnt the importance of working in the industry while studying. University can only teach so much about architectural history, technology, communication, and design; the rest comes from working in practice. There is mutual benefit;

Photography — Lisbeth Grosmann

students bring youthful enthusiasm to the workplace and take what they learn in practice to influence their student work.

Learning architects don't know everything

When I started university in 1994 the local economy was coming out of a recession. There were not many opportunities available; however, I think it's become even harder to find student work now. I made a few calls to practices that, as a general rule, didn't take on first year students. As a practitioner I can now see why—they wanted students to have more exposure to the industry and the culture of architecture.

I was offered a student position during second year with a practice in Fitzroy, ITN Architects, a co-operative of four architects who worked mainly on residential and hospitality projects. I primarily worked with one director, Aidyn Halloran. My desk was located next to his and I would hand draft mark-ups listening to his phone conversations with contractors, builders and clients, which was valuable exposure to the practice of architecture. Solving problems, negotiation, construction jargon—all things we take for granted after years of practice, but new to an architecture student. That experience influenced my practice; locating newcomers to the studio next to my desk as there is much you can learn aurally.

My first introduction to a construction site while studying was working for the in-house construction company at the Prince of Wales in St Kilda, building a 40-room boutique hotel and day spa. I assisted the construction manager and, being based on site, I met with trades daily to discuss construction issues, order materials, and chase up orders. I was dropped in the deep end and learnt a lot in two and a half years.

The experience taught me the importance of collaboration, working with trades, utilising their knowledge for the benefit of the project, and knowing that the architect doesn't know everything.

Starting in practice

Having worked with Wood Marsh as a graduate architect for three years on various complex residential and multi-residential projects, I had a desire to start my own practice. I wanted to be the author of the work rather than just a contributor. Again, the learning curve at Wood Marsh was steep and formative. I was fortunate to be given a large amount of autonomy to contribute creatively, which is really important. As architects working for other architects we're not simply draftsmen; we need that creative outlet and to have an opinion.

I thought that starting my own practice would give me more personal freedom with having a family; it does, but it comes with other demands of running a business. As an employee I would have taken maternity leave; however, this wasn't possible with my own practice. Projects overlap and run for a long time, the studio needs guidance and input. Architecture is a demanding profession and the nature of the work makes it challenging to run a practice part-time. Clients need regular follow-up contact and guidance, and builders on site can't wait. I often brought my babies into the office for the first six months, scheduling meetings and appointments around their sleep times. You make it work the best you can.

Architecture isn't unique; finding work-life balance in all professions is the Holy Grail.

It's better to work collaboratively than instructing people exactly how things should be done.

Brick House
Craving privacy from looming neighbouring flats, two new structures were conceived to cocoon a private central courtyard. Designing for your own family is a challenge, especially when the builder is your husband. Ideas tested in this project have informed subsequent projects, and gave us a greater understanding of the emotional journey our domestic clients take.

The big obstacle is guilt; you're either not committing enough time to your children or not committing enough time to the office. I've learnt to set boundaries with both, having children forced me to work more regular hours.

Moving forward

I didn't start practice with an architectural commission; rather I ended up accumulating numerous small interior projects. I didn't have a website, there was no social media, I hadn't photographed our work, but business grew organically by word of mouth. Within the first year I realised it was becoming increasingly busy as I was running thirty-two small projects. I needed to find larger projects and reduce the quantity. It's important to step back and assess from time to time, to refocus and recognise that sometimes you have to say 'no' to work and people. I've been through that process again this year. After 11 years of growing organically, it's now about growing strategically.

Targeting larger projects potentially halves the number of jobs on our books while still giving us diversity if any are put on hold. We still love working on select small projects as these give us an opportunity to test ideas that inform our other work. The right balance for us now is a mix of small, medium and larger projects. The challenge is not having too much work and overloading the office, but not having too little either.

Beautiful reward

I'm grateful for the relationships and friendships I've formed in the industry, and sharing the highs and lows with those colleagues and friends. There is a fantastic supportive architecture network in Melbourne that I feel a part of.

Seeing a building come together on site is the reward for months of work. There are many factors in the making of a project and the design and documentation process is long. The brief, site constraints, budget, sustainability, and design response all push and pull the project in different directions. It is about finding the balance between these elements that makes for a great project; as well as collaboration, trust, and patience.

Our best projects evolve from a great relationship with the client. Trust leads to great outcomes.

As the build progresses and structures start to look like a building, there is a great sense of excitement. I love seeing the client's anticipation transform to delight.

— *Does the influence of nature remain the most important consideration in design?* Nature's influence is multi-faceted. It might be how people occupy space; different generations or different family units. It could be about the materiality of projects, and the sustainable qualities or life cycle of a building. All of these things are points of focus in our practice.

Considering how a building is occupied now and in the future is an important thought process for our studio. Even though we're often designing bespoke houses for a particular client, we keep in mind how the building can be adapted or provide flexibility for the same family in years to come, or new occupants. For us, the materiality of the building is something

Photography — Shannon McGrath

Photography — Shannon McGrath

Photography — Shannon McGrath

Photography — Shannon McGrath

that's considered from the very beginning. We use a limited material palette, seeking clarity in the design. I'm drawn towards honest materials; materials utilised in their natural state, unadorned or unfinished. The natural qualities of the materials provide interest and identity, avoiding the need for applied decoration. Materials used in their natural state have a robustness which should age well.

Construction is one of the biggest consumers of product and building materials, and producers of waste. There is a responsibility for the broader profession to practice responsibly, to salvage, reuse, restore, and to build quality design that will last. There is too much poorly designed, poorly constructed, disposable building stock in our cities.

Architecture for all

A misperception exists that architecture is an elite service and profession. Good architecture thinks beyond itself. It considers the implication in the immediate surrounds but also more broadly. Architects are problem solvers and we should draw upon our design thinking skills. We need to educate the wider community about the benefits of architecture. Too often architecture is thought of as an optional extra, frivolous and expensive. Good architecture is about people, it's engaged, and can transform communities. It focuses on listening to the needs and wants of users and is contextually sensitive. The challenge is how we communicate this more effectively, to make architecture accessible to the broader community.

Rising above commonplace

An even measure of knowledge and inspiration is important; one should not outweigh the other. Architects learn until the end. I gain more understanding and knowledge in the profession each day, which is inspiring. I learn from doing and also from observing others in architecture and other creative pursuits. There is such creativity in Australia which encourages us to do better with each project. Inspiration comes when I'm in the right mindset. When I'm busy and stressed with deadlines my mind is closed to inspiration. I'm most inspired when I have time and my mind quiet —then the most banal things can be inspirational; the view from my car window, a scene in a film, a book.

— *Does the present education system really measure up?* I can't comment specifically on the content of education, but students are graduating without setting foot inside a practice. It is essential for students to work in the industry while they study. Working in the profession exposes students to everyday practice; drawing standards, communication, documentation, product knowledge. Practice also sheds light on dry tertiary subjects like professional practice, which cover insurance, liability, GST and progress claims—essential knowledge for registration and running a practice.

Practitioners need to recognise that students and graduates need to be mentored, educated, and exposed to the variety within practice.

— *What advice would give a student when they hit a brick wall?* Don't give up and try a new approach. Whether it is employment-related or solving a design problem, there are many ways to approach things. Talk to friends and colleagues to see whether they have any suggestions; there is much to learn from other people's wins and losses.

— *Is the best education studying buildings rather than reading textbooks?* Books and photographs are one thing but experiencing buildings in person is another, which is why architects live to travel. A photograph of a building won't evoke the sensory experience of a building; whether it's cold, the smell, the sound of the wind, the spatial experience. There's no substitute to experiencing a building in person.

It's important for architects to be better advocates for the profession and demonstrate the value they can bring.

—— What qualities do you look for when hiring for your practice?
I'm blessed to have a talented team of ten. They are engaged, dedicated and thoughtful. Creative and technical ability are necessary, but it's important we enjoy each other's company and work collaboratively, so personality is an important factor in who we employ. We like graduates and students in the office to have guided autonomy on their own small projects. Everyone jumps in to help each other. It makes for a rich outcome when there are multiple authors on a project rather than just one director.

Radical transformation

Architects design in three dimensions; however, representation was traditionally in two-dimensional drawings and hand-drawn perspectives. This only gave clients a sense of the project. Not everything is resolved at the beginning but we're finding a greater demand for visualisation for the client to thoroughly understand the building—often too early in the process of design. There needs to be room for the design to adjust as it develops.

The obsession with computer imagery has led to the decline of the hand sketch. The ability to sketch an idea or solution on the spot with a builder or client is a powerful tool.

Architects seem to have taken a step back in the construction phase of our built environment, particularly on larger projects when novated to a builder and replaced by a project manager. There are numerous factors that need to be managed during the build; budget, time, quality, integrity. It is important for architects to be better advocates for the profession and demonstrate the value they can bring.

St Kilda East House
Involves a series of insertions woven into the fabric of the original building. Exploring the tensions between old and new has been a keen interest of ours since the beginning. While these projects are now a smaller proportion of our work we love their complexity; a sympathetic response to the existing fabric requires another level of consideration beyond just site context.

Life Lessons

14

Clare Cousins

- Sometimes you need to say no to move forward
- Forge collaborative relationships to push boundaries
- Architecture isn't an elite profession, it is a community service
- Build adaptability and future use into your thinking
- Use honest materials in their natural state
- There's no time to waste, just get on with it
- Share knowledge with the next generation
- An architect's role is to learn until the end

Abbie Galvin

No perfect way

Abbie Galvin is a principal at BVN, one of Australia's largest and most highly-acclaimed architectural practices. Among her portfolio of work are the Taronga Zoo Upper Entrance Precinct, the Braggs Research Institute, the UTS Campus 2020 Masterplan, the HMAS Creswell Redevelopment in Jervis Bay, and the Royal North Shore Hospital.

15 / 20

Abbie is a member of a number of advisory panels including those for UNSW, The University of Newcastle, and the Eminent Architects Panel for the Sydney Opera House. Abbie has worked for over 20 years on public, educational, health, research and workplace projects that have been recognised internationally for bringing fresh approaches to common project types.

She is a firm believer that building typologies benefit from exposure to other sectors, that experts in their field always have something to learn from the amateurs and that the core of innovation comes from cross-disciplinary expertise. This openness and fresh thinking is emphasised by her recognition that there is no one perfect way to achieve great design.

There Is no right in architecture, no perfect way to solve a problem, no correct answer.

National Life Sciences Hub (NaLSH), Charles Sturt University
Playing a pivotal role in reshaping the campuses Science Precinct, the National Life Sciences Hub (NaLSH) is a teaching and research facility for the life sciences at Charles Sturt University, Wagga Wagga. The NaLSH is the first built project from the Science Precinct masterplan developed by BVN. NaLSH provides a hub for research and education in plant and animal sciences, food production and security, animal health, and water and environmental sciences. The building is designed to link students, academics, researchers and technical staff both within the University and externally with industry.

From the ground up

As children we took for granted the views of our gardens from large windows and the peculiar finishes in our kitchens and bathroom. We thought it was entirely normal for someone to have on their shelf a porcelain oyster tin with the lid rolled back revealing twelve pert porcelain breasts. An awareness of the built environment and design was always quite omnipresent as I grew up but in a fairly unassuming way. It was something I imagined was similar for everyone. My father was an architect, and our old timber house was in a constant state of construction. The walls were full of artwork and shelves full of potter's pieces. Two close childhood friends who lived nearby had similar experiences. One lived in an old house that had also been simply renovated by her architect father, and the other's house was a wonderful modern, yet modest architect-designed, red brick courtyard house. It was full of a large and somewhat avant garde art and sculpture collection. It wasn't until I reached high school, and met friends who came from established waterfront suburbs, that I realised we were slightly unusual.

No-one else had lime green rubber floors in their kitchens, or mezzanine platforms built in their bedrooms, or painted coal tar creosote on their fences, not just to keep away the white ants but as an aesthetic finish. That being said, I wasn't driven to be an architect. In many ways, as I got older, I was in awe of the creative process associated with design, and slightly intimidated by it. Ultimately, just as design and a consciousness of the built environment were implicit in my life, choosing to study architecture felt a natural choice.

Photography — John Gollings

Radical perspectives

There is no 'right' in architecture, no perfect way to solve a problem, no correct answer. I studied at the University of Western Australia, which at the time was going through a pretty radical transformation in its design teaching approach. Simon Anderson and Geoffrey London steered and enabled an environment of fantastic experimentation. The Renaissance notion of the architect as the artist/sculptor awaiting creative inspiration was totally shaken up. They gathered a dynamic range of design tutors from across Australia and the world, many practising architects, and opened the field for quite radical experimentation. As students, we moved from one studio to the next, testing and working with different approaches to our design problems. From creating buildings out of perspectival shifts, to slicing, splicing and twisting known works of architecture into new works of architecture, to traditional romantically based approaches to form and place—it was a whirlwind of trials and tests.

I remain eternally grateful for such an intense design education, for having my mind opened to the many opportunities in design approach, and for having the right environment to begin to find my own way.

Photography — Christian Wild

HMAS Creswell Griffiths House

Griffiths House is located on the site of HMAS Creswell in Jervis Bay, and provides short-term accommodation for Officers of the Royal Australian Navy undertaking leadership and management training. HMAS Creswell, established in 1915, has major national heritage significance and the site is characterised by elegant white-washed weatherboard buildings.

Photography — Christian Wild

In our need to give attribution to the single genius, we dangerously over simplify the creative process.

Here I began to understand how personal architecture is. How our thoughts and ideas are laid bare—naked almost—to such public scrutiny. In addition to the public critic, there is the self-critic who is often even more powerful. Everything we do is ultimately an experiment at some level, a personal approach to programme and place, an uncovering and interaction of tacit understanding.

It is a continual interplay of feeling and reason. I also began to understand that the more I learnt, the less I knew. How could one possibly ever grasp the significance of the role we have, the tasks we have ahead of us, and the enormity of what we need to know. Neither of these things have left me. The personal being so public will always remain difficult for me, while I continue to be aware of how much I still have to learn. I find this one of the most energising aspects of what we do.

— *Was it tougher for women back then?* 'Back then' appears to be a term that should be posed to another generation. I don't feel like I've had a 'back then'. However, if I reframe the question as 'Has it been tough as a woman in architecture?', I'd say not at all. To be honest, I was never aware that my gender created any issues for me. I went to a co-ed high school and there was never a focus on girls being able to do anything they chose. The focus was on all of us to do and achieve. The only discriminator appeared to be between those who were and weren't prepared to work hard.

At university half the year was female and consistently represented among the award winning students in every year, but again it was never really a talking point. When I began working in architecture I was never conscious of my 'femaleness' —the acute realisation was my youth and inexperience. There was always an expectation that as young architects we didn't know much. I've used this to my advantage over the years by asking lots of obvious and awkward questions that many others were too embarrassed to ask. I still do a fair bit of question asking—it's a great way to learn.

Unsurprisingly, the challenges for women hit as we begin to have children, and until we see childrearing as a joint responsibility this challenge will remain. Anne Marie Slaughter (director of Policy Planning for the US State Department) said at a talk in Sydney recently: "we need to stop talking about women when we talk about children," which of course involves a significant cultural shift. In addition, there are structural issues within our industry, in fact within many industries, about speed and rapidity of performance.

Expectations are increasing about how quickly we deliver and perform, which puts burdens on everyone and impacts the amount of time we spend working. Ultimately, I think the only way we, as a society, are going to enable women to sustain participation in a meaningful way in the workforce is to have a fundamental change in our approach to work. Work/life balance simply cannot be a woman's issue. It must be an issue that faces men, women, the old, the young, those with family and those without.

Freedom to be

I'm not sure whether I would ever describe architecture as giving me 'freedom'. Freedom is the absence of necessity or constraint in our choices or actions. Architecture, while it has incredible breadth and opportunity, involves a constant process of synthesising necessity and constraint with knowledge, intuition and understanding.

I think architecture does provide an extraordinary opportunity to explore and experiment with thoughts and ideas and ultimately to have those thoughts and ideas built. This transformation from the drawn idea to the built object is among the most mind blowing, humbling and at times terrifying experiences. I still pinch myself when a building or a space begins to form. Recognising that someone has had enough confidence in us to let this happen is the ultimate privilege.

Rising above commonplace

There are lots of moments when it feels like bits of the roof fall. Horrible feelings where my gut hits the floor, or my chest constricts, but they're generally momentary. The reasons vary—sometimes it's realising I've made a vital error, or one more project adds to the deadline pile, or a wonderful colleague leaves, or I forget something critical that I needed to do—I've worked out that I have to write everything down these days. The worst ones are when I feel like I can't work something out, where the challenge or problem is insurmountable. I'm a big deep breath taker. It's amazing what a deep breath can do to enable you to refocus. However, I've found the most productive way of rebuilding those bits of the roof is to talk them through with someone. My husband is also an architect, and he, along with many of my trusted colleagues are great sounding boards and fantastic critics. Sometimes it just needs the voice of another, someone unencumbered with all that I feel encumbered with, to turn me in a different direction. My advice would be to never battle on alone.

Architecture has so many layers of complexity, from the technical to the mundane to the poetic, and attempting to respond to everything at once can be debilitating. There needs to be clarity and intent in generating the idea. Whether it is about materiality, context, place or creating experience—which can enable a form of yardstick to measure decisions and solutions and options by. Finding a 'way in' can sometimes mean thinking about small pieces rather than the whole, it can be about research and reading about the place, the site, the history or the programme. As the saying goes, 'Eat the elephant one bite at a time'.

HMAS Creswell Gymnasium
The HMAS Creswell Gymnasium is the physical fitness facility for the Royal Australian Naval College located in Jervis Bay, NSW. The Gymnasium successfully merges two seemingly conflicting requirements: providing a large and robust facility for demanding naval training that nestles discreetly within a spectacular and historically significant natural setting.
Photography — John Gollings

Life Lessons

15

Abbie Galvin

— There is no one perfect way to achieve great design

— Knowing you can never know enough energises every day

— Eat the elephant one bite at a time

— Architecture is not a solo endeavour

— Never battle on alone

— The core of innovation is cross-disciplinary collaboration

— Experts always have something to learn from amateurs

— Computerisation is not the idea

I do believe architecture is becoming increasingly emblematic. We are at risk of trivialising and not assessing the less-visible qualities of architecture in favour of the image.

Taronga Zoo
Taronga Zoo is an iconic zoological garden in Sydney's northern city suburb of Mosman. The Upper Entry Precinct project delivers a major entrance and car park for the zoo, which serve to restore the emphasis on the natural beauty of Taronga Zoo's setting and resolve issues with traffic flow and people movement.

Photography — Brett Boardman

And leading on from my previous response about falling roofs—take a deep breath, and find someone to run your thoughts by—architecture is not a solo endeavour.

Immersion and inspiration

In our need to give attribution to the single genius we dangerously over simplify the creative process. We assess architecture from many aspects simultaneously—aesthetically, historically, functionally, personally, emotionally—but the design process also works at simultaneous levels. It is a continual interplay of feeling and logic, between relational and rational thought, and allows intuition to sit alongside reason with impunity. Knowledge and memory layer with the consideration of the functional and the technical. However, I am immediately drawn to the place as a starting point—the power of what's around us. The aim being to create a building that has an aura of its intended place and a relationship to its context; be that an urban, spatial, historic or a social one.

Working with others in a genuine dialogue, one that is truly immersed in discussion and interrogation, can also be inspirational. Too often architecture is seen as a sole endeavour, when in fact it is mostly one of extraordinary collective participation. Musician Brian Eno coined the word 'Scenius', "... the intelligence of a whole, of an operation or group of people". It suggests an ecology of talent and ideas that create a quality of work more indebted to the friction between collaborators than to the work of any single artist. I am continually appreciative of the intellectual, creative and technical talent that surround me.

Thinking space

I do tend to think best at home, sitting at the dining room table, looking out across the bush and the harbour. The space is lovely and the light is. It's not so much the physical space itself that creates the right atmosphere, but how it embodies calm and the removal of time and pressure of the day-to-day. I think one of our increasing problems is the expectation of speed—the sheer pace of response can become almost debilitating. We have all sorts of tools and systems in place to make our production easier and faster. Rather than using that time saved to allow exploration, testing, review and quiet thought, we give it away. We are seduced into producing more and we focus on the image; not on an authentic and considered response to space and place.

Radical transformation

I think one of the biggest shifts in architecture has been a plethora of information now available to us regarding what's happening in architecture globally. We used to see new projects—built work or schemes—via physical journals or books. Once the monthly or quarterly journal arrived in the office, the work itself was generally a number of years old, and always carefully curated and selected. The articles were devoured, and images, drawings and text scrutinised. Now of course, we don't just see careful editor's selections. We are bombarded with endless images of projects that are happening globally, the very moment they are complete, and often when they are just conceived. We are now part of a wonderful global community, but at the same time, the volume of information shared has increased our rate of consumption and, arguably, the way we process and interpret it.

We're undoubtedly in a world where amazing opportunities exist. I think the limitations occur when computerisation is the idea. There are numerous examples of buildings that have been about cleverness and novelty over significance and longevity. I believe architecture is becoming increasingly emblematic. We are at risk of trivialising and not assessing the less-visible qualities of architecture in favour of the image.

The Braggs, University Of Adelaide

The Braggs houses the Institute for Photonics and Advanced Sensing (IPAS) and an undergraduate teaching facility at the University of Adelaide. It incorporates both research and undergraduate laboratories, and a 420 seat lecture theatre. The central philosophy of the building is to enable researchers from different scientific disciplines to come together to enable a transdisciplinary approach to research.

Photography — John Gollings

Ingrid Richards

Future history

Operating in her home town of Brisbane, Ingrid Richards co-founded Richards & Spence with the aim of choreographing vibrant public spaces from private commissions. A graduate of the University of Queensland, Ingrid was an associate with Cox Rayner Architects before commencing private practice in 2008.

Richards & Spence projects are broad in type, ranging from furniture and restaurants to hotels and large scale urban developments with a focus on urban infill retail. The practice participates in the public realm through a predominantly commercial clientele. Operating in a close-knit community of retailers, restaurateurs and business owners, they are subject to the accountability of local use. Ideas of custodianship and legacy apply equally as they do to public commissions. Across the following pages, Ingrid shares a little of her design journey and her practice's motivation to reconnect commercial interests and the community in the heart of our cities.

16 / 20

19 James Street
The commission for 19 James Street required the building to be reorientated to participate in the successful streetscape, mending the existing network of streets and lanes and offering a hierarchy of retail frontage. Cross-block connections to neighbouring sites are galvanised with a finer grain of retail experience. The result establishes a pedestrian network rather than creating an object for its own sake.

I believe that the accumulation of buildings over the history of a city is not only desirable but necessary if buildings are to embody our collective memories and aspirations.

From the ground up

I come from a family who for the most part are historians and teachers; the readers and writers of books. My father was a hard-working company man who instilled in me at a young age the importance of having a 'profession'. My mother is a genealogist, an avid reader and the centre of all knowledge. My parents had both been denied a tertiary education, my father as a young ex-serviceman and my mother due to it not being considered appropriate as a female. Both insisted on the fundamental importance of education and there was never any doubt that I would finish school and go on to university. The vocations of my older siblings include a museum curator, a teacher of the deaf, an academic historian who specialises in Australian indigenous history, a psychiatric nurse and an agronomist who became a park ranger. Always encouraged to find our own path, we independently followed careers with humanitarian tendencies. Settling on a profession in architecture seemed to me the right balance of design creativity and social conscious.

I fell into architecture thanks to the advice of a friend who had started the course and challenged my understanding of it as a dry profession for old men. I studied at University of Queensland under the 'Old School' tutelage which included, John Macarthur, Michael Kenniger, Greg Bamford, Britt Andersen, Peter O'Gorman, Ian Sinnamon and Max Horner. Of these many are no longer with us or have since retired. My education was rich and, at times, brutal—it took me years to appreciate its depth.

During the compulsory year of work experience after my third year of architecture, I had my first opportunity to travel overseas and experience the life of European cities. Every street, plaza and park I went to was fantastic, occupied at all hours, by every kind of person, engaging in social interactions I had previously only associated with private home life.

Until this point, architecture was a speculative thing—an abstract design exercise—and the potency of this experience remained for a long time at odds in a Brisbane context where the possibility that the 'ordinariness' of fruit and vegetables retail might become a delightful daily ritual was a revelation. After travel, my final years of study took on a new focus and application as I embarked on the James Street Market project while at Cox Rayner Architects (winning the 2003 National Award for Commercial Architecture, AIA). In order to prioritise experience, the scheme proposed basic urban elements: a public and pedestrianised 'street', a central courtyard and an inward-facing market hall and in doing so challenged conventional retail format.

The reality of these ideas taking on a physical, built form became a fiercely motivational force. In a close-knit city where family, friends and colleagues were assessing my work, the weight of responsibility felt very real. In the end, the reward in having had a hand in delivering an everyday food market was the contribution of a place in my own neighbourhood which had personal value and meaning.

Starting in practice

It was a conscious business decision to tackle the much maligned typology of retail, in which we recognised the potential for reinvention.

Going into private practice with my partner, Adrian Spence, in 2008, coincided with a personal decision to remain in Brisbane. We set up our practice in the optimism of that period but by October the world had run out of money. I had left a secure job in a period of intense bullishness for private practice in a time of doubt.

In mid 2009 things were looking up again as we embarked on a large retail market project. It was a dream brief and also seemingly stable, with site, approvals and funding secure. By 2010 we were commencing documentation with our newly hired staff, when the local council resumed the site and the project was stopped without warning. In our first two years we had accrued two intimate experiences of the unpredictability of the construction industry.

Early projects included hospitality; a school building; and, most commonly, commercial refurbishments. The commission to design 19 James Street was our first major adaptive reuse of a building in the James Street retail precinct. Our approach to the commission was to re-orientate the building to promote participation in the streetscape and mend the existing network of streets and laneways, galvanising cross-block connections to neighbouring sites. In a city where historical streetscapes are rarely found intact, we were compelled to make a building with civic gravitas. Our aspirations were to convey a sense of longevity of construction, character and occupation, while contributing to the vibrant retail enclave.

Project work following 19 James Street continues to explore opportunities to make buildings, which satisfy a range of public and civic functions. As a means to understand those enduring qualities

Photography — Toby Scott

Photography — Alicia Taylor

West Elm, Pottery Barn
9 Wandoo Street acknowledges historic precedent by adhering to a reduced material palette of brick and concrete while providing an autonomous framework for the ever changing shop window. An overlay of landscape located on the roof preserves precious ground level space. The resulting built form reinforces an enduring streetscape precedent to create 'future history'.

It was a very conscious business decision to tackle the much maligned typology of retail, in which we recognised the potential for reinvention.

Photography – Toby Scott

of public space, we look to historical precedents. Gallerias, markets and malls are all examples of 'ground based' retail systems, which celebrate a hierarchy of public space as extensions of the plaza, square, street, laneway, arcade and courtyard. As well as being places of economic exchange, they support civic interaction and are conduits for movement in and around the city. Assessment of these places has led us to determine that good public space satisfies basic and common criteria, which we simplify to be: accessible to all, safe and the harder to define element of charm. Another way to judge the same set of criteria might be to question whether the place is suitable for a first date. Is there a level of comfort and safety? Is there an endearing element of delight?

We prioritise streets over buildings. In parallel we seek to orchestrate an experience driven by the delight of the interior over the awe of the exterior.

Many of the projects that have come out of our office were initially questioned: the cork interior of the Survey Co. Restaurant; the white bricks at 19 James Street; and, the raised cactai garden at 19 Wandoo Street. The strongest reaction is generally reserved for the arch, a cry of 'It's too 1970s', suggesting the system was first invented in the suburbs of Brisbane rather than prehistoric times.

All of these elements aroused a strong reaction out of a small portion of people coming to terms with materials and forms remembered from their youth. Others liked it immediately and some didn't care. I like to think that people should be challenged and can come to appreciate an approach if it is delivered with good intentions. I don't believe in buildings intended to

Photography — Toby Scott

shock, they are usually a one-liner and are quickly boring. Memories, deeply embedded, should be tapped into.

Beautiful reward

A building is its own reward and no amount of training can prepare you for the wonder of a project under construction. It also comes with a sense of self-doubt, a questioning of 'how could this have been better?', which leads to any number of sleepless nights. But then without reflection there would be no improvement. It is a fine balance of questioning one's work while remaining confident in one's own decision process.

Having your own business affords many freedoms. The greatest of which is who you choose to work for and with whom. In an architectural setting this extends to opportunities to guide your practice towards areas of particular interest. For myself, the establishment of Richards & Spence followed the completion of three projects at Cox Rayner Architects: James Street Market (2003), Ferry Rd Market (2007) and All Hallows' School (2007). These projects were an evolution of ideas developed over a decade, which explored opportunities to layer civic and social programme within private settings. A pivotal moment in my own thinking, and an encounter I shared with Adrian, was the prodigious experience of visiting 'C House', the famed work of Timothy Hill and Brian Donovan. It struck me as a great tragedy that one of the most important examples of local, 20th century architecture was not a public building. If I was going to remain in Brisbane I wanted to make spaces I could continue to use. Since public commissions seemed unlikely we looked to retail and hospitality for this brief. By trusting our 'gut feel' we have been able to develop a strong business model alongside an artistic and cultural agenda.

Progressing the profession

We are experiencing a renewed focus on accountability. This is particularly significant in a city like Brisbane, which is minor on a world scale but where presently many building projects are underway. At some point we must ask ourselves what our legacy will be from this time of relative prosperity—the best buildings or the most buildings? On one hand working in a 'new' city allows great opportunity for architects. The stage has not been set and there is literally room to establish a new context. The flip side is the absence of precedent, the eternal challenge of the 'blank canvas'. This has resulted in some odd buildings, each aiming to stand out from its neighbour, each aiming to be memorable. I am interested in a counterpoint to the hype surrounding 'newness'; we are working toward enduring solutions for buildings in a rapidly evolving environment.

I believe that the accumulation of buildings over the history of a city is not only desirable but necessary if buildings are to embody our collective memories and aspirations. How better to understand the idea of collective identity than through our built structures; elements that we don't need to own to be able to share in, buildings that mirror our civic identity and buildings that ideally, we can be proud of.

Rising above commonplace

Travel is the ultimate inspiration. We travel often and never fail to return invigorated. Curiously, however,

Life Lessons

16

Ingrid Richards

- Architecture is not an abstract design exercise
- Private commissions can achieve community outcomes
- Find opportunity in humble commissions
- The experience must be prioritised over the image
- Professional tenancity is key
- Artistic and cultural agenda can operate alongside a strong business model
- Architects must be held accountable for future precedent
- Seek ‘endurance’ over ‘newness’
- Question your work while remaining confident in your decisions

The whole becomes more valuable than the sum of its parts. A future history emerges. These places become ingrained in the fabric of the city, held together by a collective memory, evolving over time.

Photography — Toby Scott

The Survey Co.
At the heart of the scheme is the dining room, kitchen and bar. A terrain of cork tiles defines the interior reappropriating a material historically found in the domestic domain. A schedule of custom steel doors and windows, robust with deep reveals, delineate openings and create places for wine display. Brass is used sparingly in custom designed furniture, light fittings, handrails and signage.

I am not a comfortable traveller and am frustrated by the experience of watching others 'live', while I remain, essentially the voyeur. While away I am always thinking about how a particular place or detail could be applied 'at home'.

— *Do you think the present education system measures up?* Education is crucial; providing historical background, technical skill and theoretical outlook. It is important, however, to remember that an architectural education may lead to many other professions. Lateral thinking is critical to architecture, and also in the skill set of divergent fields. I think the ability to look at something from many angles and to approach a project impartially and reasonably is perhaps the best indication of a successful graduate. I remain in two minds as to whether school leavers should go directly into the course as a strong basis for learning or commence with additional personal experience. However, regardless of timing, I believe critical to architectural education is a focus on problem solving and more importantly, questioning the problem itself. If every graduate gained experience through the resolution of a nuanced built outcome, our cities would improve exponentially.

— *What qualities do you look for when hiring for your practice?* We aim only to hire emotionally functional people. There is no place in architecture for those who do not feel compassion and remorse. Of course this is coupled with a requirement for technological knowledge however no amount of learning can make you inquisitive or responsible. I would place leadership and tenacity at the forefront of architectural success. Building projects take time and the drive to see it all the way through is paramount. Unless the team is galvanised and able to stay the course, it is unlikely the result will be anything other than mediocre. For this reason, we also like working with and for people who are positive and kind. It doesn't cost any more and makes each day a whole lot more enjoyable.

Radical transformation

Louis Kahn said, 'architecture must concern itself primarily with the anatomy of society, and therefore with its institutions—churches, synagogues, universities and museums.' Whether retail precincts, the accessible ground plane of offices, restaurants or bars, in reality we spend much of our time within these commercial spaces and they make up most of our urban fabric.

Despite increased access to architecture across the world, whether through images or travel, there is a renewed focus on local relevance. This is not immediately recognised on the majority of large projects where conservatism is a natural outcome of a nervous global market. The risk of offending or not appealing to all is too great—however with this comes the risk that the resultant building does not really appeal to anyone.

What is important, is that the image—whether a render or photograph—is not prioritised over the experience. I think that the real experience of a building, monument, or landscape should far exceed any expectation that can be captured in a still image. This is equally the case for the work of Álvaro Siza as it is for Uluru.

Our practice works on the basis that there is scope to make a good public space out of a private commission. These are highly commercial endeavours and many of them are not glamorous. The smaller retail developments in particular are largely overlooked, often seen as low-end architecture and not at all aspirational. It is these elements that we must pay special attention to—the privately owned places of public interface that people use every day.

As we embark on the James Street Hotel project—our fourth major commission within the James Street Precinct—we begin to appreciate the importance of having a consistent architectural agenda. With each new building bound to and strengthened by the one before, we witness a progression of our neighbourhood and a maturing of our city.

The whole becomes more valuable than the sum of its parts and a future history emerges. These places become ingrained in the fabric of the city, held together by a collective memory, evolving over time.

Photography — Alicia Taylor

Photography — Alicia Taylor

Annabel Lahz

Holistic hook

Annabel graduated from the University of Queensland with Honours and received the Queensland Institute of Architects Medallion, the Board of Architects Prize and the University Medal. Before establishing lahznimmo architects in 1994, she worked at Lindsay Clare Architects and Lawrence Nield and Partners Australia.

17 / 20

Annabel is known for her ideas based approach and considers architecture to be a balance between the pragmatic and the conceptual. She is particularly interested in the intersection of landscape, urban design and architecture. Annabel believes architecture is a tactile and visual medium. It should respond not only to its site context but also to its cultural and social contexts creating environments and experiences, which enhance the daily lives of their users. Here we get a feel for her lifelong pursuit of that often-elusive holistic hook.

Centennial Parklands Amenities
The male and female programme was divided into two pavilions linked by a continuous roof. The space created between the pavilions acts as a central entry point to the amenities. The hand washbasins are externalized as a polished concrete trough and are located in this central communal space providing a unique experience for the user to wash their hands and look out to and still fee a part of the activity in the Park.
Photography — Brett Boardman

From the ground up

I was fortunate from the beginning as my parents were very interested in all types of design from furniture through to architecture, art and fashion. They had eclectic tastes, enjoyed beautiful things and were very progressive in their thinking. So it was fairly natural to develop an appreciation for design and art from an early age.

While growing up in Brisbane we lived in three contrasting houses. The first was a classic timber Queenslander raised off the ground on stilts; the second was a classic 1960s; and, the last was a contemporary architect-designed, subtropical house commissioned by my parents. Looking back at these houses now from an architect's perspective—although stylistically different—they had common themes revolving around being well designed, well constructed and detailed, and above all very liveable. Growing up in these environments heightened my awareness of why good design matters. I can't say that I had any epiphany or eureka moment that architecture was my calling. I can remember tossing many different professions around in my youth from artist through to a vet or marine biologist. My focus however through school was mainly art based, I vaguely envisaged some sort of career in the arts through painting and drawing. My mother was pivotal in my decision to do architecture rather than fine art—primarily she advocated for architecture as it was a profession so I would have an income. Given this was the main basis of my decision-making, I was very lucky in that the architecture course at the University of Queensland (UQ) just clicked with me almost straight away. I have been on track ever since.

The Go-betweens and everything in between

The education I received at UQ provided a strong foundation to my design approach and the way I think about architecture. University was still free in the 1980s and so attracted a diverse range of people. While the department gave birth to many architects it also was a breeding ground for other creatives including bands such as the Go-betweens. The 'studio' in those days was always populated with

I was fortunate from the beginning as my parents were very interested in all types of design from furniture through to architecture, art and fashion. They had eclectic tastes and enjoyed beautiful things and were very progressive and modern in their thinking. So it was fairly natural to develop an appreciation for design and art from an early age.

someone almost day and night and was both a social and workspace. Perhaps it's nostalgia but I remember my time in the early 1980s as being a golden period for the UQ architecture department, then was under the stewardship of Michael Keniger—an Englishman who studied and taught at the Architectural Association in London (AA), as well as academics such as Brit Andersen, Peter O'Gorman, John Macarther and Don Watson. We were given a grounding in the sensory aspect of architecture as well as introduced to west coast American architects such as a young Frank Gehry, Greene and Greene, Bernard Maybeck and Rudolph Schindler.

The presence of Michael Keniger provided the school with a connection with the Architectural Association (AA) in London and we would get a steady stream of AA academics such as Peter Salter, Peter Cook and Alison Smithson. They would come to Brisbane in our summer to escape their winter, providing us with an international perspective of current architectural thinking, which was seen as a cultural backwater compared to Melbourne and Sydney. Education was always something my parents held in high regard and when the opportunity presented itself to go to the AA in London in my fourth year they were very supportive. I was fortunate enough to be accepted into Peter Wilson's unit back in the day when Peter's career was in its infancy and he was relatively unknown. The impact of this year is still with me. Peter introduced me to the role of the narrative and the figurative in architecture and how this can imbue a building with its own sense of life and character. He also showed us the importance in speculation and the role that humour, wit and playfulness play in architecture.

Starting in practice

We have often referred to lahznimmo as literally 'stumbling into existence'. Similar to many young practices, we started off

Tamarama Beach Kiosk and Amenities.
The new design respects the deep feelings of the community ownership of the park and beach by providing for the community's needs, and reflecting the unique character of the local community.
Photography — Brett Boardman

Wallace Wurth Redevelopment for UNSW Medicine (lahznimmo architects with Wilson Architects).
The central atrium space provides visual and physical connections becoming the School's social and community focus. The space is defined by a series of velvety tangerine rings as well as an ever changing pattern of sunlight and shadows creating a sensory and tactile experience for the occupants. Photography — Brett Boardman

Life Lessons

17

Annabel Lahz

- A site's context is not only physical but also its social and cultural memory
- Developing a meaningful 'narrative' for a project is key
- Architecture is as tactile as it is visual
- Beware the 'narcotics of patternmaking'
- Speculation, testing and challenging traditional ideas and approaches fuels innovation
- Architecture should be for 'mutual benefit'
- Playfulness plays a salient role
- Time is elastic but final deadlines aren't
- Look for the holistic hook

Photography — Brett Boardman

Bowen Place Crossing
The design response is fundamentally landscape driven. The new underpass is part of a continuous path that slices through the terrain on a trajectory that speaks to the existing geometries of Bowen Place and the National Carillon.

Photography — Brett Boardman

Design is our most valuable skill yet it is constantly undervalued both by our clients as well as ourselves.

as a husband and wife team. After the birth of our twin boys and taking a year off work to look after them I returned to work. This allowed Andrew to resign from his job to look after the boys part-time, as well as starting our practice. The decision was an easy one to make as we realised we would be financially no worse off as the cost of childcare equalled one of our salaries. So with nothing to lose we eased ourselves into private practice. It was about two years before we had the critical mass of projects for me to join Andrew full time. Similar to many architects our first commission was our own house alteration and additions, which we comprehensively photographed and published to establish our design credentials. From there we have slowly transformed the firm over a twenty-year period. We've outgrown the "husband and wife" tag; taking on new creative partners to become the architectural practice we are today—a practice defined by the quality and creativity of our work.

Beautiful reward

In our practice turning twenty years old there was a massive sense of satisfaction and achievement. To mark the occasion we collated a book *LNXX—lahznimmo architects a twenty-year retrospective*. The book itself became a vehicle for us to pause and review our body of work and identify the recurring themes, which run through our projects. We described the book as 'part reflection, part celebration and part contemplation of the future.'

Seeing a project take shape is ultimately the greatest reward. There is always a little bit of nervousness and your perception of a project under construction is constantly changing, as the construction progresses and moves from slab to structural skeleton to fully skinned. It is really not until the scaffold comes down that all is revealed. The scaffolding always seems to be up for so long but then comes down so quickly. It's very exciting and there tends to be a real buzz around the site as everyone, from the client to the subcontractors, gets a real feel for exactly what it is they have been working on.

My biggest high is when the client has moved in and the spaces are being used the way we envisaged, as well as other unintended but often delightful ways. The ultimate is coming back to a project a few months later and your client telling you how much the building has met (and ideally surpassed) their expectations. Even better, being confronted by the naysayer who complained throughout the design process and who grudgingly admits the outcome is in fact terrific and thanks you for standing by your ideas.

Progressing the profession

Design is our most valuable skill yet it is constantly undervalued by our clients as well as ourselves. As a profession we are at a crossroads—a point where our role is changing and we need to use this as an opportunity to reinvent ourselves. I think the most pressing issue for architects is the need to redefine our role in the building process. Over the past few decades the architects' control over the design and building process has been steadily decreasing. While there will always be a handful of (starchitects) the vast majority of our built environment is procured through multiple variations of design and construct models. These are designed to minimise risk for the client—minimise costs and time. Increasingly architects are unfortunately engaged by the building contractor rather than the client, which removes us from direct communication with the client and the major decision-making. There is also a trend towards fewer firms and larger firms as well as multi-disciplinary engineering firms with inhouse architecture departments. Smaller to mid size practices struggle to compete against these larger practices, which can offer more competitive fees; a one stop shop service as well as a sense of security for the client by virtue of their sheer size and breadth of the portfolio. This conservative trend towards risk reduction and a more corporate approach to our built environment has contributed to stunting innovation in our profession and increasingly pushes architects to the periphery of the building process. It has also contributed to a dumbing down of architecture where many buildings are given a vapid 'look' without a clear rationale behind them.

So one of the key questions facing the profession is: 'how do we remain relevant in a more corporate system as well as achieve good design outcomes?' If we return to fundamentals it is 'us' architects who have the 'smarts'. It is us who provide strategic thinking, design problem solving, conceptual approach and materiality to buildings and the built environment. No other profession does this better than architecture. We need to advocate more effectively about the importance of good design not only to our clients but also at a city, regional and national level. We should not give away our ideas for free if we expect them to be valued.

My prediction is that over the coming years we will see a push back against corporatised architecture with a move towards more diversification within the profession and more emphasis on the quality of design, whether it be to a developer's bottom line or to the public. On larger scale projects I see architects taking up the role of 'facilitators', positively taking part in the process of reducing costs and achieving deadlines while still advocating the benefits of good design. Smaller practices working in the public realm will increasingly collaborate with larger offices as well as position themselves as 'design and strategy' experts.

I think there will also be more hybrid firms. These firms, in addition to pursuing architecture, will seek out other disciplines to collaborate with on other types of design-projects. This could involve collaborating with artists; industrial designers; packaging; graphics; theatre productions; lighting; temporary structure specialists. This model is fuelled by younger architects and recent graduates becoming increasingly frustrated by the

Armory Wharf Café, Blaxland Riverside Park Sydney Olympic Park Authority
The design draws extensively on the industrial landscape and military themes of the site utilising a broad palette of materials such as, weathering steel, army camouflage netting, recycled timber, and mill finish aluminium. Within the café functional necessities of kitchen exhaust and gas flues have been encased in a chimney structure that also playfully references the silhouettes of retained cranes. It is this dialogue that we seek which is both pragmatic and poetic.

It is to be hoped that these younger fringe dwellers actually make their way back into the profession to assist in its renewal.

profession and looking for more creative outlets. This can only be invigorating for the profession, encouraging experimentation and interdisciplinary collaboration. Interestingly it seems to be encouraging larger more corporate practices to have in-house research and innovation hub to maintain their cutting edge and progressive images. So perhaps we might come full circle.

Rising above commonplace

Inspiration can sometimes be elusive and I find that speculation is a remarkably important part of the design process. Speculation and testing different ideas, as well as challenging current thinking are part of how we innovate as architects and develop new solutions. There is never only a single solution for a project. Speculation can also be just allowing your mind to wander down different paths and rabbit holes discovering accidental possibilities as you go.

— *Does the present education system really measure up?* Like many architects I have interviewed my fair share of undergraduates and graduates. Generally I consider that most of our universities are out of step with the realities of the profession. Traditionally there has always been a strong link between the academy and practice, with working architects being central to teaching. This is shifting towards full time academics and doctoral candidates, which skews the emphasis to teaching. Of course university should be a place for dreaming and making up imagined forms and environments, however this needs to be tempered by the realities of practice.

Photography — Brett Boardman

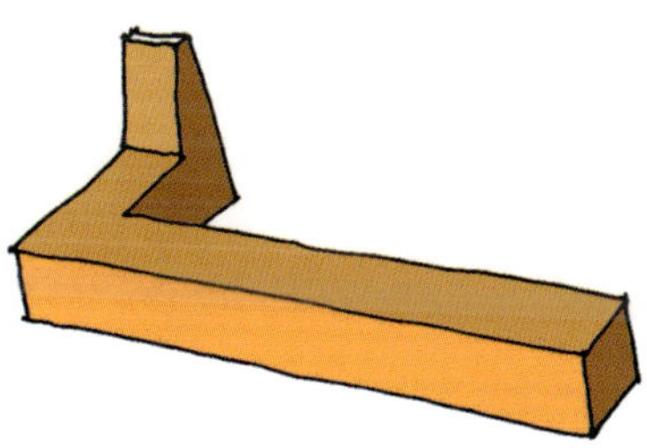

Many graduates are starry eyed—some lucky graduates will find homes with design-based firms, but the majority will go into large practices with limited opportunity for dreaming and meaningful design input. For many graduates this will not be a problem as their skill set might be more suited to the challenges presented. However there will be some who will feel disenfranchised. Many frustrated younger architects either leave the profession entirely or move sideways into innovative hybrid firms with a variety of design disciplines. It is to be hoped that these younger fringe dwellers actually make their way back into the profession to assist in its renewal.

— *What advice would you give a student when they hit a brick wall?*
Stop:—think and ask yourself 'what's the story, what is my project's narrative?' If the answer is you don't have one or you don't know what it is then you need to go back to the beginning and search for the drivers for your design. Often, you will infact find that you have a narrative driving your project, only you have forgotten it or deviated and lost your way.

Early on in my career, Professor Lawrence Nield would often refer to the 'Narcotics of pattern making' in architecture. By this he was referring to the 'addiction' that architects develop to endlessly churn out different facade patterns unrelated to the building's function or context. Whenever I feel myself stray into this dangerous territory I can hear those words echoing in my subconscious and steering me back to asking the question 'why does my elevation look like that?' There must always be a reason otherwise you are in the realm of 'the narcotics of pattern making.'

Is there a common DNA running through successful architects?

It would be great if we could genetically engineer the ultimate dream architect. They would have the following attributes: resilience; optimism; persuasiveness; equal amounts of confidence and humility; measured and thoughtful; talented and creative; business acumen; charisma; gravitas; an accomplished orator; technically savvy; and, able to produce beautiful hand sketches. Sadly genetics isn't at this advanced stage and I think this is why good architects are the sum of their parts, which is to say their co-collaborators.

I would like to think that increasingly as we move forward, architects take on this social contract to create architecture, which has mutual benefit in a more serious and responsible way.

Photography — Brett Boardman

Warragamba Dam Visitor Centre and Operations Complex (VOC), Sydney Catchment Authority
The building has two primary addresses: Haviland Park and to the Spillway and Dam wall. Firstly, from the Haviland Park side the landscape is emphasised and the building is downplayed. From the cliff side however the building is more expressive and hovers dramatically on the edge of the cliff face with a series of public viewing platforms. The expression of the building draws on the scale and engineering heroics of the Dam and Spillway.

Radical transformation

Architecture the good; the bad, the mediocre and the ugly, is everywhere creating our environment and providing the backdrop for our lives. The biggest obvious shift since starting out some thirty years ago is going from the drawing board to the computer, and more recently to BIM modelling. I love today's capacity to do three-dimensional modelling. Though I hate to admit that I am a bit of a Luddite. I don't actually do the modelling myself and I often sit beside someone in the office looking at options. We utilise software throughout the project from sketch design through to construction. It's the ultimate visualisation tool not only for the architect but also for the client.

In parallel with this transformation are also a variety of technological advances in how we access information and communicate with one another: mobile phones; the web; email and myriad of social media. But these are all physical changes and perhaps more profoundly, for our profession, are the social and political changes that have impacted not only on the architect's role but on our built environment. Good architecture has the potential to enhance and transform our lives while poor and mediocre architecture either contributes little or can have a negative impact on our lives. Architecture plays an immense role in creating liveable cities. For architecture to be given this opportunity there is a responsibility on architects to design thoughtfully and responsibly. Equally for policy makers; developers and government to understand and see the mutual benefit in good design. I would like to think that, as we move forward, architects take on this social contract to create architecture that has mutual benefit in a more serious and responsible way.

Christina Na-Heon Cho

Cross-cultural creativity

Christina is an Associate at Cox Architecture in Brisbane. Continually widening her horizons, Christina's creativity is underpinned by a philosophy of participatory democracy, driving change throughout the global design community and wider society.

18 / 20

Christina studied architecture at the University of California, Berkeley and University of Queensland, where she graduated as Vledictorian with First Class Honours. Christina has a diversity of experience having worked for Duga Architects (Seoul), HOK (San Francisco), and Donovan Hill (Brisbane), before joining Cox Architecture in 2010. Her work includes a wide variety of projects ranging from residential, education, health, institutional architecture to commercial construction and masterplanning. Her work also extends to public art installations. She collaborates with designers in Seoul, Tokyo and London under the name Rice Cake Mafia. Rice Cake Mafia's projects include the winning entry in a global competition for Tokyo Designer's week, public commissions for the Museum of Brisbane and for the Brisbane Powerhouse. Christina draws from her multi-cultural background to facilitate dialogue and encourage the community to think differently about placemaking and the influence of culture in the transformation of our cities.

Architecture gives you the ability to work with people across diverse platforms, to be creative problem solvers, to be thinkers, to design, create, make, and facilitate.

Photography — Christopher Frederick Jones

Exploring new territories

What drew me to architecture can be summarised in one of my favourite quotes, which appears in the Bauhaus manifesto: 'the ultimate aim of all creativity is the building.' To be a good architect one must practice with a balanced knowledge of artistry, craftsmanship, sociology, history, engineering, anthropology and the environment. Architecture gives you the ability to work with people across diverse platforms, to be creative problem solvers, to be thinkers, to design, create, make, and facilitate. It's city-making, the home, public and private, the formal and intimate. I love that architecture is all of this and more.

Life at the cultural crossroads

I've been fortunate to have lived my life at the crossroads of two unique and wonderful societies. I was born in Seoul and raised in Brisbane. My Korean-Australian heritage has significantly shaped the way I view the world and, consequently, my work in architecture. I was immersed in a rich background of culture, history, politics, arts and tradition. Both influenced by my mother's background as a ceramic engineer, educator and writer, and my father, who is a political historian and academic.

My parents took an immense risk—just as Seoul was preparing its global debut to host the 1988 Olympic Games—and packed up our possessions, and relocated to Brisbane so that my father could pursue his doctoral studies. His thesis was on the reunification of North and South Korea and the move to Australia gave him access to restricted books and information not available in the South. I spent my summers at home flipping through the pages of tomes on various subjects from political discourse to contemporary Asian art and acupuncture. To this day, my imagination continues to be challenged by books on every subject imaginable.

I am a third generation architect. My grandfather was a graduate architect during the Korean War and was conscripted into the army to design bridges and military facilities. After the war, he started his own firm

University of Queensland Oral Health Centre
This building abstractly conveys its purpose embodying the 'craft of dentistry'. It enriches it context and humanises the institutional building at every moment in its experience.

and became the first architect to be registered in his province. He named his practice "Guk Il" Architecture, meaning 'One Nation'. My uncle followed in his father's footsteps and took over the firm after my grandfather's death. Growing up in Australia I did not have direct exposure to their work, but the term 'architect' has always been familiar and relatable.

I have inherited a love of culture, arts and music from my mother. My mother's mother was a hanbok designer (traditional Korean costume) and my aunt trained as a traditional dancer and musician. She was the protégé of a Korean living national treasure. My mother also has a great passion for teaching. During my youth she taught at the Korean Language School on Saturdays—sharing her knowledge of Korean art and traditions with Korean children and their adoptive Australian families. She viewed it as a way of holistically nurturing the children to embrace their Korean ethnicity and heritage. My mother and I immediately connected with these families. We still continue to gather and rekindle the learnings from the classroom over my mother's home-cooked Korean feasts.

These life lessons of creating meaningful connections and finding opportunities to share cultural dialogue play an integral role to my work in architecture, design and making.

Horizon lines

When it came time to decide what to study at university I selected architecture as it was familiar, relatable and challenging. I wanted to better the world and architecture gave me the fundamental skills to be a creative problem-solver and make a meaningful contribution to the world.

My definitive 'line in the sand moment' was my time spent studying and living in San Francisco. Berkeley opened my mind to new ways of thinking. While studying I became a member of the DECAL (Democratic Education at Cal) Committee. DECAL is a student run education programme which provides Berkeley students the opportunity to study from a broad range of student-designed courses that promote critical thought, self-discipline, community and responsibility. There was a distinctive notion in which people interacted with one another. Hierarchy and authority were rejected and knowledge was spread horizontally from peer to peer.

This notion has influenced the way I practice. My approach is to strive to be progressive, leading the conversation but to also share knowledge, and engage in dialogue between all those who are involved in the project team and community. In my mind, the architectural process is not complete until it leads to informed and reflective action. I choose to have faith in humankind, my colleagues, and in participatory democracy. Respect, openness and kindness are key values that permeate all aspects of my life.

Starting in practice

I have observed and learnt from the work of many incredible minds over the years. I've come to understand the different roles an architect can perform in the shaping of our cities. How it can extend beyond the pragmatics of the building, to create platforms for community engagement and dialogue. After graduating from university, my first job in architecture was at Donovan Hill. Timothy Hill and Brian Donovan worked with a strong

Ipswich Government Office Building

This first stage was stimulated by the Queensland Government's policy of regional decentralisation and city centre activation. Focus is placed on the vibrancy of facades and ground level interfaces to generate urban renewal vitality, which can be enriched as future buildings and spaces are developed. The corner entry canopy opens up the formerly impenetrable corners of the precinct and aligns with the historic Post Office opposite.

Life Lessons

18

Christina
Na-Heon Cho

— Cross-cultural appreciation enriches design

— Initiate innovative and socially responsive solutions

— Reading heightens a curious mind

— The ultimate expression of creativity is building

— Immerse yourself in different cultures and cities

— Approach every opportunity with an open mind

— Bring people into the problem solving process early

— Practice your values and ideals in every aspect of life

St Aidan's Anglican Girls School
The first stage of the Innovation and Design Hub was a small classroom extension made from contemporary white brick to complement the original brick buildings in the precint. The small scale project presented an opportunity to experiment with traditional materials in an unconventional way, as well as detailing to inform key design elements for future stages of development.

Development is necessary. However changes have to be realistic, respectful, and ones that reinvigorate and sustain our community.

design philosophy and conviction. They promoted an office culture which valued socially engaged architects. It didn't matter if the project was within a private or public realm - each job acknowledged, addressed, and enhanced existing physical and social conditions.

There, I met James Davidson. An incredibly generous architect, and a former Director of Emergency Architects Australia. In 2011, floods devastated our state, with nearly two-thirds of the land under water. It was James who rallied architects to volunteer their time to inspect and assess thousands of damaged homes, offering support and advice, and building a sense of community in its greatest time of need. When you initiate interactions, and lead with purpose, energies can be directed at collective outcome for greater positive change.

At Cox Architecture I am inspired by our directors and senior colleagues who are ambitious and resilient. They transfer their ideas and knowledge with patience and humility. They entrust responsibilities and give young architects, such as myself, the opportunity to refine our design skills and lead projects.

Our directors encourage and support staff to make greater contributions within and outside of the profession. Their personal commitment acknowledges that balance is required for both professional and personal growth. This culture of support has enabled me to continue my involvement with EmAGN, FutureNet, and PechaKucha Night as a means to facilitate and catalyse dialogue, and engage with greater effectiveness with the community, industry and government.

Freedom to be

Architecture involves utilising a broad range of fundamental skills and knowledge. It is not limited to the physical construction of space.

This breadth of knowledge has enhanced my understanding and ability to learn more about society and its relationship to the built environment. My curious mind constantly seeks and craves inspiration. My side projects include explorations of ways to trigger human conversations and interactions that activate public space. I have collaborated with designers based in Brisbane, Perth, Tokyo, Seoul and London on public art installations. These projects are fun, quirky, and allow me the freedom to experiment and re-energise my passions for architecture outside traditional practice.

In my final year of architecture school, my friends Kirstie, Luke and I started PechaKucha Night Brisbane, bringing the creative forum from Tokyo. PechaKucha is now held in over 930 cities, and presents an up-to-date snapshot of the local creativity from cities around the world. It is part of a truly global conversation. PechaKucha Brisbane provides a platform for creatives from diverse backgrounds to collectively learn, share, and exchange ideas. Nine years on, we have curated 46 events and over 460 creatives have presented their work. Most importantly, PechaKucha created a platform for members of the community to engage and continue dialogue on their cities, as well as inspire and be inspired.

Beautiful reward

Great architecture is the result of the creation and communication of ideas from many talented minds. From the skills of the design architect, documentation and detailing team, collaborative efforts of engineers, landscape, interiors, graphic designers, visualisation staff, through to the builder, indispensable trades and craftsmen.

Each project presents a new challenge. I find joy in working with people to come up with creative solutions to complex briefs. I want to keep creating beautiful spaces even under pressure. Mountains can literally be moved when the construction team, consultant team and creative all work with the same purpose in mind; to create a great building not only for the end-users, but also a building the city and its people will value.

Ultimately, I find delight in my architectural and design practice. Whatever the project may be, I strive to create happy outcomes. My side projects and involvement in the community sustain my passion and keeps me curious to continue learning.

Progressing the profession

Development is necessary. However changes have to be realistic, respectful, and ones that reinvigorate and sustain our community. Construction is inevitably a major catalyst in environmental degradation. It is responsible for a large part of the world's energy consumption, emissions and landfill. It is critical for each profession in the built environment to adopt and implement sustainable strategies now to steer the direction of development. Ideas exchange needs to occur between a greater scope of disciplines including science, technology, law and economics. We need to adapt our design and construction methodology with new technologies and passive strategies. Architects have a shared responsibility to stimulate new perceptions and challenge ingrained ideas.

Daniel Libeskind once wrote, 'one can put a book away, but a building and the city are always present across time, across history, the art of building itself transforms the city.'

Projects have the ability to change the framework of the city and its skyline. I recently worked on Kings Square in Perth. It was designed as both an extension and intervention to the CBD. Projects on the scale of Kings Square change the cityscape.

It helps when clients themselves are visionaries and open to exploring and experimenting new concepts.

Photography — Hyojin Kwon & Christina Cho

It changes the way a city is connected and the experience of the pedestrian. I imagine the multiplicity of ways people will eventually use the spaces we have created and how it will shape the city. It fills me with energy and resolve to bring these ideas to life.

Rising above commonplace

When the humdrum becomes overwhelming, I am reminded that I still have much to learn. I delight in the challenge I have to raise awareness and understanding of the role architecture can perform in shaping our cities

Textbooks form a good foundation and appreciation for architecture. You can learn about the history and theory behind a building, which may not be readily apparent on the face of the building. However, in order to fully appreciate a building you need to have a clear understanding of the city as a consequence of its collective historical, cultural, and social existence.

When the opportunity arises, travel to and experience cities that have transitioned through centuries of political, religious, cultural and industrial movements. Experience life beyond the threshold. Explore, observe, and experience the city through human conversations and interactions, and learn from the social dynamics of the city. You can see beyond the pragmatics of the building—it's more than the lines on a page. You also experience first-hand the quality of space, light, materiality and scale. One finds clarity when they experience the building first hand.

— *What advice would you give a student when they hit a brick wall?* It's not a brick wall. You've reached the crossroad which will influence you in ways you can't begin to imagine. The discoveries we make and the impact we have, often find their sources at our past crossroads. So keep challenging yourself and underscore the importance of pursuing passions by answering your own questions with first hand experiences. Most importantly bring other people into the process. People become empowered to better understand and solve problems when they have support. By way of example, while I was at Berkeley, one of our projects was to design

Intersect—My Own Private Neon Oasis
Collaboration with Hyojin Kwon as Rice Cake Mafia. Commissioned by the Museum of Brisbane as part of its contemporary art project, "My Own Private Neon Oasis". Intersect's form focused on the integration of the diverse cultures and identities in Sunnybank, a predominantly East-Asian suburb in Brisbane. Taking a light-hearted approach, the design integrated a Chinese Dragon and Australian Kangaroo in bamboo, wrapped in native sarsaparilla vines.
Photography — Hyojin Kwon & Christina Cho

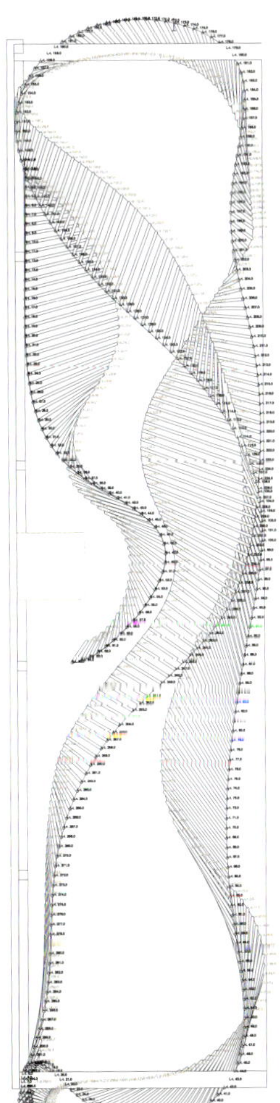

Branch Out—Brisbane Powerhouse
Collaboration with Hyojin Kwon as Rice Cake Mafia. A quirky upside down Christmas tree composed of 365 branches and ornaments. The back of each ornament is scribed with a handwritten message that embeds meaning and personalises the object. On the last day of the exhibition, all ornaments were gifted to people so that the memories and materials were sustained.

and construct an emergency shelter prototype. We learnt that there were limits in architecture—cost, site, programme, and construction. However, our biggest lesson was the ability to identify these limits as opportunities as architects to influence the design process to engender innovative, socially and environmentally responsive solutions.

Architecture is a powerful tool for social change. As an architect, you are designing for people-shaping conditions for life. I hope that all young architects leave university with strong values and commitment towards progressing humanity and strive to become the type of well-rounded and socially engaged architect the wider world will value.

Radical transformation

As a 'Gen-Y' architect, the Global Financial Crisis (GFC) represented the first major economic downturn in our careers. Since 2008, the majority of development has been fuelled by the private sector. I've noticed that projects from government and public institutions have dwindled since the GFC. I wonder when my colleagues and I will have the opportunity to design and work on great public spaces which our predecessors worked on and left their mark on the city.

The traditional model of boutique practices have given way to larger amalgamated full service firms as many become absorbed or integrated in order to remain economically viable and maintain a strong market presence. While in some ways it has forced firms to innovate in order to remain competitive and take projects on a global scale, I wonder how sustainable this trend will be if it continues unchecked.

Furthermore, I've noticed the number of graduate architects has almost doubled in Queensland with the opening of two new architecture schools. As is the case with many young professionals, there are sadly not enough jobs in architecture firms or government to go around. As a result, graduates are branching out into related fields like industrial design, project management and development. While some lament this turn of events, I am excited about the cross fertilisation of ideas and spreading of architectural knowledge to other industries. I think it will ultimately make our work as architects easier as we will all start with the same appreciation for design and place making. It helps when clients themselves are visionaries and open to exploring and experimenting new concepts.

Kerstin Thompson

At home in the world

Kerstin Thompson is principal of Kerstin Thompson Architects (KTA)—a Melbourne-based architecture, landscape and urban design practice with projects in Australia and New Zealand. She is an advocate for architecture in her role as member of the Office of Victorian Government Architecture, Design Review Panel, an occasional writer, curator, and jury member.

19 / 20

Committed to design based research and education she is currently Professor of Design in Architecture at Victoria University of Wellington (NZ) and Adjunct Professor at RMIT and Monash University. KTA projects span a range of sectors and have been extensively awarded and published. Her focus is on architecture as a civic endeavour with an emphasis on the users' enjoyment of place. This chapter explores KTA's projects as portraits, unique and particular to the client, community, context and environment at hand.

House at Hanging Rock
Capturing vistas of vineyards and rural pastures, the house unfurls over a series of terraces. The upper terrace forms the main bedroom suite, the middle terrace living with kitchen and dining areas, and the lower for studio and guest use. Its concrete palette integrates BAL requirements while its attenuated form extends gracefully into the landscape.

I've always been drawn to the restorative potential of architecture: to rebuild a sense of community, to repair an ecology, to mend an urban fabric, to create environments that invite people to connect with themselves and to each other. The best architecture constantly finds ways to do this.

Photography — Trevor Mein

Photography — Sharyn Cairns

Early intuition

Becoming an architect stems from an early intuition about the importance of creating a sense of home. Rather than 'home' as a specifically domestic condition I mean 'home' as the physical framework required for each person, (alone or with others) to feel supported in their day-to-day activities, whether in the private or public sphere. The making of this quality, of being 'at home in the world,' motivates me as an architect.

Architecture is the combination of people and place. My fascination with both—and how they are mutually defining—is a constant inspiration for making buildings and landscapes. As is my belief that architecture can make a demonstrable difference to our quality of life.

Starting in practice

I initially gained experience working with several practices including the Ministry of Housing, MMH and Mattheo Thun in Milan. Then, as a preamble to my thesis, I worked for a year with Robinson Chen Architects, and importantly, builders too who over about a decade produced a handful of excellent houses in Melbourne. I admired their work and so somewhat presumptuously dropped into the office one day hoping for a student position. I managed to get a five-minute talk with Kai Chen who skimmed my folio with little interest. What he intuited was an attitude. He was less interested in what I knew and more in what I could learn. So began my year there which though brief was a concentrated, high quality time—the most formative of my pre-KTA professional experience.

I spent a lot of time on site, which I loved. It was exciting and immediate. From this I also saw the complexities of being builder and architect; the meat-in-the-sandwich relationship to clients, and the stress and risk of building and designing on the spot. I came to value the discipline of the traditional contract documentation set, the necessity to make your call in the drawing and only in crisis to redesign in the medium of bricks and mortar.

What made it such a formative experience was that it helped me understand what I valued. How I wanted to practise with design integrity but also with a degree of work-life balance. With fair pay and reasonable conditions being parallel to architectural intelligence and delivery. To make a practice where people could be themselves.

Moments of consequence

In 2014, the House at Hanging Rock won the Robin Boyd Award from the Australian Institute of Architects. Australia's pre-eminent housing award, which recognises 'the most outstanding work of residential architecture in Australia,' it's an honour to have achieved this recognition.

As a woman architect, however, I have consciously sought a focus on public projects as a direct challenge to aligning women and specifically women architects more with a domestic rather than civic sphere. While I am greatly honoured to have received the highest of accolades for our housing work I am also delighted to have also received considerable recognition, through awards and publication, for many of our public sector projects including the Monash University Museum of Art and for institutions such as the Victoria Police.

The good bones of a building will orchestrate the nature of the relationship between public, private and common space, between one home and the next. These are the kinds of challenges we need to focus our collective architectural intelligence on.

Carrum Downs Police Station
KTA's suite of police stations demonstrate the way a generic programme can be adapted to suit unique site contexts. Reflecting the shifting culture of the Victoria Police as a community rather than an institution we developed an alternative plan typology for Carrum Downs. Imagined as a mini city, the station comprises of a cluster of programmatic elements each figured as an individual volume, treated materially as a building and distinguished through a particular choice of brick, a material that in turn references the domestic buildings that skirt it. The inclusion of internal courtyards allows light, ventilation and aspect to interior spaces while maintaining privacy and security to the external street facades. While the station is predominantly low in form the entry tower shifts the scale of the facility from domestic to civic, and as an illuminated beacon at night, heralds the presence of the Victoria Police on the highway.

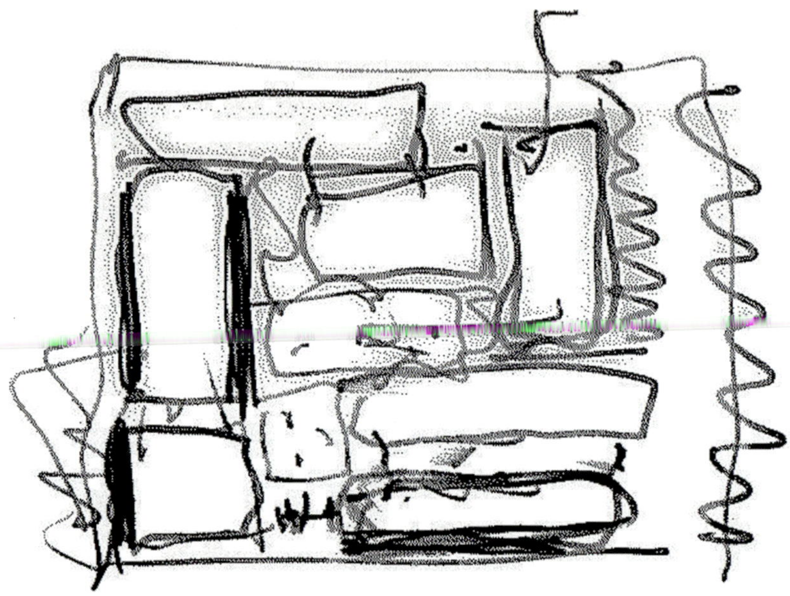

Photography — Peter Bennetts

Photography — Trevor Mein

This involves encouraging even the most private projects to provide a public benefit and support community life. Broader questions need to be asked about the way buildings are designed. How does this building contribute to its neighbourhood? Is it kind to its neighbours? Does it increase the quality of the street it's in? Is what's being proposed better than what's already there?

Fundamentally there needs to be a greater understanding and advocacy of the role of architecture and design, an appreciation not just in terms of what it looks like but what it can do. Design has the ability to connect or separate people, and it can do this in unexpected ways. The street front of a museum can either welcome in the surrounding community or sever ties with it. The floor plan of a home, by the mode of circulation it adopts or the number and arrangement of bathrooms relative to bedrooms, can significantly influence the way a household relates, whether more or less connected.

The design of workplaces can also nurture collaboration and influence the way colleagues relate to each other. In the five police stations KTA has designed, we've explored the way subtle design changes be used to connect various functional divisions to encourage sociability and exchange of information between them. This is also a question of the way architecture and new developments relate to their surrounding environments. The extent to which a new building overshadows its surroundings or alternatively harbours green and generous spaces for community gathering can be influenced by design choices.

Take the recent debate around high-rises in Melbourne. The focus of commentary—on whether the cultural reference for the face or body of the building is appropriate—is a distraction away from the more critical question facing Melbourne's multi-residential industry. That is, how to develop alternatives to the prevailing type, defined by deep floor plates and continuous skin? At a minimum we must increase levels of amenity, especially the basics of light and air in habitable rooms and a relationship to the public realm.

In this sense, the focus needs to fall on building typology. Put simply: the bones of a building set up a pattern for subdivision, configure dwelling types, define the building envelope and establish an interface with the street and neighbours. These, I would argue, more crucially transform how we might live with or near others and in our cities and suburbs.

Monash University Museum of Art and Ian Potter Sculpture Courtyard
What was a disconnected collection of buildings overrun by cars is now a vital, calm oasis. The museum engages with the distinctive geometry of the original building to bring the inside out, drawing the art into the landscape to enhance the campus grounds and provide a cultural focus. The introduction of a major canopy provides a threshold for events including after-hours museum openings and cross-campus links.

Hill House
Celebrating the shadow in the making of home, this house continues KTA's interest in dark space, the heightened sense of intimacy and mystery for domestic life that this affords and the retreat it provides from the harsh Australian sun.

The shift from sketch to working drawing to lived space is a transformation that continues to inspire my wonder and delight.

Gender parity

The question of gender parity in architecture is a complex one. In order for women to be recognised for their work they need to be given equal opportunities to actually do the work in the first place. So far this opportunity has not been equal for a variety of reasons. If there is a lack of parity in roles then this can be accounted for by cultural prejudices embedded and played out in day-to-day practise, in subtle and not so subtle ways. In my experience it is important to be aware of gender roles. 'Girls do interiors, boys do technical'—it goes something like that. Actually girls do towers too and boys select curtains. So it's essential to maintain vigilance around gender-based expectations and how you represent your practice and the kinds of jobs you choose to work on. It's important to embrace them if they fit, or resist if not. Personally I hope to be respected as an architect—full stop. Not a woman architect. Similarly I hope that the buildings we design are judged by the criteria we may expect to apply to any architecture not a special one reserved for women architects.

I certainly do not ascribe a gender to our buildings and am always somewhat perplexed when people remark that they find them 'masculine'. How did they determine this? Something to do with straight lines and at times direct use of materials, which can apparently be attributed to the masculine rather than feminine.

As a practitioner I am more acutely aware, I think, of the language and concepts that frame and describe architecture and the extent to which these are overlaid with gender bias. It's important to be mindful of this in the thinking we bring to bear upon our buildings. After a lecture once, in which I showed a project I described as an interval building—one wedged between two iconic towers—I was asked if this was a possibly feminine response. I certainly think an interest in building as an interval stems from my late 1980s Postmodern/post-structuralist education which involved the rethink of classical oppositions in architecture.

Rising above commonplace

Inspiration really only counts for 5% of the outcome. The other 95% comes down to critical rigour and careful thinking about how inspiration might be acted on and made into something real.

Still, inspiration and learning knows no bounds. I find it unconsciously in the day-to-day especially while walking. More directed inspiration I find in other buildings, their siting, approach to context, the precedents they set, examining them as case studies and reflecting on the lessons learnt from their design and construction. Also the informal nuances of a brief, the implied rather than the explicit, often hold precious nuggets for architectural opportunity.

Music and literature also trigger new thinkings around a problem. And like architecture they come about from an iterative process of drafts and redrafts. Like architecture they provide an immediate pleasure as an experience but also as a conceptual structure. You want to be able to listen and enjoy but also know there's something organising and driving them.

— *Does the present education system really measure up?* Nothing is pure in architecture; it's messy and imperfect so teaching students how to productively engage with the messy and imperfect is a really important part of education. We need to be better at training students to negotiate and deal with the contingent; to work with and in relation to each other. This way we won't think of architecture or design as the creation of a sole author but rather as a group effort. We're not sole geniuses working in a vacuum. Just as buildings aren't things that exist by themselves - they're always connected in our cities - so we need more of that interconnectivity in teaching

— *What advice would you give a student when they hit a brick wall?* Look again at the work of others, perhaps a favourite project. Is there something you can learn from this to help unlock your own problem? Talk to a colleague. Draw it out. If all else fails go for a walk. Mini roofs metaphorically fall in on a regular basis but you realise you can always rebuild them and get back on the horse. What you think is a big deal at the time is something you deal with and then get on with it. That's how you stay in an industry for thirty years; you're not going to let one roof falling in stop you. Laughter and humour help enormously.

— *What qualities do you look for when hiring for your practice?* I look for an attitude and usually it's a highly intuitive process. It's less about a person's credentials, more about developing an immediate rapport with them, getting a sense of initiative and a proactive nature. In this way, it's not so much about their past accomplishments as what they might be capable of in their next role, and how they'll fit into the existing dynamic and culture of the studio. The shift from sketch to working drawing to lived space is a transformation that continues to inspire my wonder and delight.

Photography — Trevor Mein

Photography — Derek Swalwell

Aesop Emporium
KTA has designed 13 stores for Aesop across Australia and South East Asia. Aesop Emporium, the company's flagship Melbourne store, employs the singular use of spotted gum timber to create an immersive space that is intimate and visually calm. The warm hue of the timber in combination with brass sinks and lights, as well as the perforated timber screens compliment the product and provide a calm retreat from the arcade which, by contrast, is reflective and brightly illuminated.

In particular for the Marysville Police Station which has been instrumental in rebuilding the local community post the disaster of the 2008 bushfires. I liked working with and understanding the parameters of the subbies. Like how thin a skylight can be before a well-fed Greek renderer can no longer access its slimness to finish it.

Beautiful reward

The moment when a project becomes real for me is the moment when I can see the spaces in my mind's eye and kinaestheically intuit its physicality too; it's not just how that space will look but how it will feel to be in, what it will sound like, the degree of its warmth, the quality of its light.

That said, each of the stages of a project have their particular challenges and joys. The initial phase of schematic design is exciting, and the grind through design development and documentation that accompanies the shift from the crude to the resolved is especially rewarding. On-site adaptations and adjustments are fascinating, as is the building process with its material and construction demands. And the eventual occupation of the building by its users, their satisfaction with it, is immeasurably satisfying.

Having my own practice has given me the freedom to work and design according to my personal and professional values. One of the main reasons I established my own practice was to ensure I could maintain both a decent quality of life and a committed architectural practice. Having had practice experience as an undergraduate in Australia and in Italy I couldn't accept that architectural integrity comes only at the expense of a personal life and family. Therefore I have sought to implement and maintain a culture of practice that supports my team and myself in a sustainable way, generally limited to a standard working day.

I liked working with and understanding the parameters of the subbies. Like how thin a skylight can be before a well-fed Greek renderer can no longer access its slimness to finish it.

Tarrawarra Cellar Door
Located in an extension of the existing tunnel, Tarrawarra Cellar Door is imagined as an intimate space that places wine and its making at the centre of the visitor experience. Its delight derives from combining an Australian landscape setting with the subterranean charm of a European wine cellar. Imagined as warm and inviting in winter and a place of cool relief in summer, pools of natural light from above in combination with niche wall lights celebrate the subterranean character so defining of the tradition of the wine cellar and its ambience.

Of course there are some longer days but these are an exception not the rule. I also hoped for and strive to maintain a practice that accepts the whole person. Each member of KTA is valued for his or her individuality. They are appreciated for not being 'yes' people and for being comfortable expressing themselves and their beliefs in undertaking their work.

Progressing the profession

The good bones of a building will orchestrate the nature of the relationship between public, private and common space, between one home and the next. These are the kinds of challenges we need to focus our collective architectural intelligence on. Architects have always been interested in progressing humanity and that's fundamental to architecture and its purpose. There just might be slightly different ways that this progress occurs. Any good architect is constantly trying to do that. The biggest shifts have been in procurement systems; more jobs are design and construct with less traditional services. This has ramifications on how we think about and protect design value. There needs to be a greater emphasis on architecture's capacity to seek out civic engagement or opportunity.

Photography — Derek Swalwell

Photography — Derek Swalwell

Life Lessons

19

Kerstin Thompson

— Good design makes people feel at home in the world

— Girls do towers and boys do curtains; the rules aren't fixed

— Visit building sites to understand design realities

— Always create good healthy bones in a building

— Architecture isn't pure, it is messy and imperfect

— Understand, respect and reuse our heritage

— We're not sole geniuses working in a vacuum

— Inspiration only counts for 5% of the outcome

— Understand each site and building as it exists within a continuum of environment and situation

Virginia Kerridge

At heart an artist

Virginia established her practice in 1995 and has embraced a diversity of projects ranging from single dwellings to apartment buildings, extending to hospitality, retail and art galleries.

20 / 20

Virginia's work has been noted in many awards and has twice been a juror on the Australian National Architecture Awards, as well as the Northern Territory Awards and two New South Wales State Awards. She is passionate about architecture both at a macro and micro level, and has been recognised for her work on interiors, treating the design as a whole. Virginia adopts a collaborative approach with clients, tailoring the project to their needs. Site and context are used as generators for design with materiality being a hallmark of her work. Adaptive reuse is a particular passion. At heart an artist, Virginia reveals how this continually influences her life as an architect.

House in Country
In line with the ideals of Peter Andrews, who is experimenting with water systems on this property, transparency to nature is a theme in the design. The connection of the human to nature is seen as most important. The more disconnected a person is from nature, the less 'well' they are likely to be. Here is a place to regenerate the soul.

My first love was painting and art, but I was interested in applying these disciplines in a pragmatic way that worked in three-dimensions as well.

Photography — Marcel Aucar

Resonance of an artist

My mother was always interested in art and design, having painted pottery for Martin Boyd Pottery, and had studied at the National Art School at a time when it would have been very exciting. She had teachers such as William Dobell, Lyndon Dadswell, and contemporaries such as Tony Tuckson and Guy and David Boyd. I used to love the stories she would tell about this time. There is a certain magic in the legacy of these great artists and I found this very inspirational.

In architecture, I thought I could find a creative occupation that had strong connections to painting, ceramics and sculpture, which I had been enjoying immensely. Throughout my degree, and while I have been working, I have constantly been doing courses in drawing, painting, ceramics, and printmaking. They help my practice of architecture. The study of painting, for instance, opened my eyes to the exploration of colour and movement.

When I was very young I was friends with the daughter of Colin Griffiths who worked alongside Harry Seidler. We were occasionally taken to building sites, which I found strange and slightly hostile places. Nevertheless I was exposed to them and had an awareness of them. At that age I had little understanding of what it all meant. Even so, when I finished school I thought I would give architecture a go to see whether I liked it. My love for it grew slowly. I really only got the hang of it once I had a bit of experience in an office where it all became a bit more real. When I went back to university after having had a year off to work, I had become fascinated with it and really started to enjoy myself. A few of my tutors had the ability to impart the fascination of architecture and I became hooked. I am a voracious reader of architecture books with a particular interest in urban design.

Starting in practice

I worked in a variety of offices when I first started, from large offices to small. While I enjoyed the social aspect of working in a large office, I was drawn more to working on smaller projects where I was able to get a grasp of the whole project. I was interested in the detail as well as the overall picture. One of the formative jobs I had was working for a female architect in New York City (Bonnie Roche and Associates). At the time she was working on an apartment renovation for Paloma Picasso. All of a sudden I was catching cabs to the Upper East Side and being exposed to another very sophisticated world. There was a guy in the office who had worked for Mies Van Der Rohe. He made the most beautiful drawings I had seen.

Life Lessons

20

Virginia Kerridge

— More often than not in architecture small is beautiful

— Materiality creates a distinctive hallmark of great work

— No design can be entirely your own

— Study the skills of great cabinet makers and carpenters

— Building something meaningful comes from building rapport

— Adaptive reuse adds to the originality of innovative design

— Become a voracious reader of buildings, not just books

— Painting opens your eyes to colour and movement

— We can't improve on nature, but we can learn from it

Lilyfield Warehouse
The creative adaptation of a 1900s rendered brick industrial warehouse building to a family home. The heart of the design is the central garden, a space that allows the building to breathe. The blue painted render has been removed, and the original bricks are now revealed. Even though the building was not heritage listed, it has become an important part of the historical fabric of the neighbourhood.

I often think buildings look their best when they are half finished. Perhaps it's just the excitement of what is to come. When they are at that stage there is so much possibility.

He would constantly tell me how lucky I was to have got a job in their office by walking in off the street. When I returned to Australia I worked for a number of architecture firms and then decided to try working for myself. Having had the experience of observing a female running a small office, I thought it would suit my personality type—I needed the flexibility. My creativity needed to find somewhere to express itself.

The first project I was able to really express myself was the warehouse at Taylor Square; designed with structural engineer Philip Wallace, my then husband. The exposure that came with this project led to other interesting projects for interesting people, more often than not the two go together. I started to get some great clients I had things in common with. The times when I've not enjoyed myself in architecture are the times when I have worked for people that I have found I have no real connection with. Fortunately as you gain more experience people tend to come to you because they like what you do and this really frees up the creative process.

Focus on People

I am lucky that I have found an area to express my creativity that is people focused—as the people are one of the most enjoyable parts of the process. Having your own practice gives you the freedom to express your own ideas albeit with the client's interests at heart. You are able to work intensively for short periods then take a break if you like, though this can be difficult. You also have the

Photography — Michael Nicholson

freedom to draw on influences from all sorts of places. For instance, certain movies, places, people, or friends can be very inspirational. Having my own office has come with a certain freedom as well as responsibility. The best part is being able to have the ability to choose which projects you like to work on. Architecture is a multi-facetted occupation and one that enables you to become involved in all sorts of things depending on what interests you. It's also very rewarding to build up a great rapport with the people you are working with.

The realisation process

It's quite a strange experience at first. I remember that the first new house I was commissioned to design was quite a surreal process. Seeing it beginning to take shape on site was an exhilarating experience, as well as being slightly frightening. The realisation of 'Oh my God, it looks just like the model'. I always like making models for every job; particularly for a new house it is essential. It's like creating a sculpture on a massive scale. I often think buildings look their best when they are half finished. Perhaps it's just the excitement of what is to come. When they are at that stage there is so much possibility.

Transcending the ordinary

In architecture, I particularly look at the work of people whose work transcends the ordinary. There are so many great architects. My particular favourites are Peter Zumthor, Le Corbusier, and Carlo Scarpa. Practising architecture is not easy, so unless you can go with the flow you aren't going to last very long. One of my tutors at university used to make life extremely difficult for everyone. In his view if you couldn't survive his brutal treatment you wouldn't survive in the real world; you need to have grit to survive this profession. The thing that drives me to rise above the humdrum is the memory of inspiring spaces that I have been in and the way they make you feel. They vary from the Pantheon and the Colosseum in Rome; Therme Vals in Switzerland; and, the Theatre at Epidaurus in Greece. It's great to see architecture that has the ability to respond beautifully to its surroundings, or that accentuates the beauty in an inspiring landscape.

— *What advice would you give a student when they hit a brick wall?*
I haven't been teaching formally lately so I can't really comment on the current education system. I think any education system relies heavily on the individuals employed. Having a great teacher can make or break a career. Architecture is all about inspiration but you need to have a certain amount of knowledge in order to pull it off, not least about the human psyche. Inspiration is all around us but I do find traveling extremely inspiring being immersed in different cultures and learning from other people and how they think.

There seems to be a general trend in the real estate market that bigger is always better. It's almost like going to the butcher and buying meat by the kilo.

Luker Residence
Respecting the character of this 1870s Edmund Rouse designed cottage, the sense of the age and layering of the old house over time has been retained. The juxtaposition of old and new works to highlight the history of the old and the refinement of the new.

I find that the more relaxed I am the more my mind is free to think of ideas. You definitely learn more from studying a building that reading a book, although there is a place for both. Being able to walk through a building gives you a sense of the space and materiality that has so much consequence on your perception of a space. You can't get this from reading a book. But at the same time, I absolutely love reading books.

— *Is there a common DNA running through architects?* I think there probably is a common DNA running through many architects although people are all different. Just as well as I think the more diverse design can be the better. I guess to achieve anything in any field you have to have a certain amount of drive and creativity. This comes in many different forms in many different people.

Progressing the profession

There seems to be a general trend in the real estate market that bigger is always better. It's almost like going to the butcher and buying meat by the kilo. More often than not in architecture small is beautiful, but today's consumer culture tends to ignore this. However there does seem to be a sort of reaction taking place to this consumerism and greed. People seem to be appreciating quality and the handmade over the mass-market buildings available. The more people are not driven by the mass mindset, the better it will be for everyone.

I enjoy the craft of building and really admire the skill of great cabinet makers and carpenters. They are the ones that really make a great work of architecture. Architecture is such a team game that no one person can take the credit for a successful building. It is always a symbiotic mix of the right people involved at each stage of work. Making people aware that having an architect involved in the design of their building can make a dramatic effect to the quality of their experience is crucial. Developer-driven design is saturating the market. If people start to really appreciate design's collaborative nature then the future of the profession will be good.

Radical transformation

The use of the computer is just another tool in the making of a building; albeit one that saves a lot of time and helps create great images—although I still love hand drawing and model making. There is a certain instant connection that is achieved through this medium. However the realism that can be achieved through a good render is phenomenal and is another art in itself. Ultimately, nature really is the mother of invention. We can't improve on nature, but we can learn from it.

The best projects that are in a natural context always relate well to the nature around and enhance the experience. Every site is totally different, as is every client, but both the site and the client are a great source of inspiration. Since I started practising architecture I think things have vastly improved. There are more women practising, more awareness of world resources, and a greater interest in public architecture.

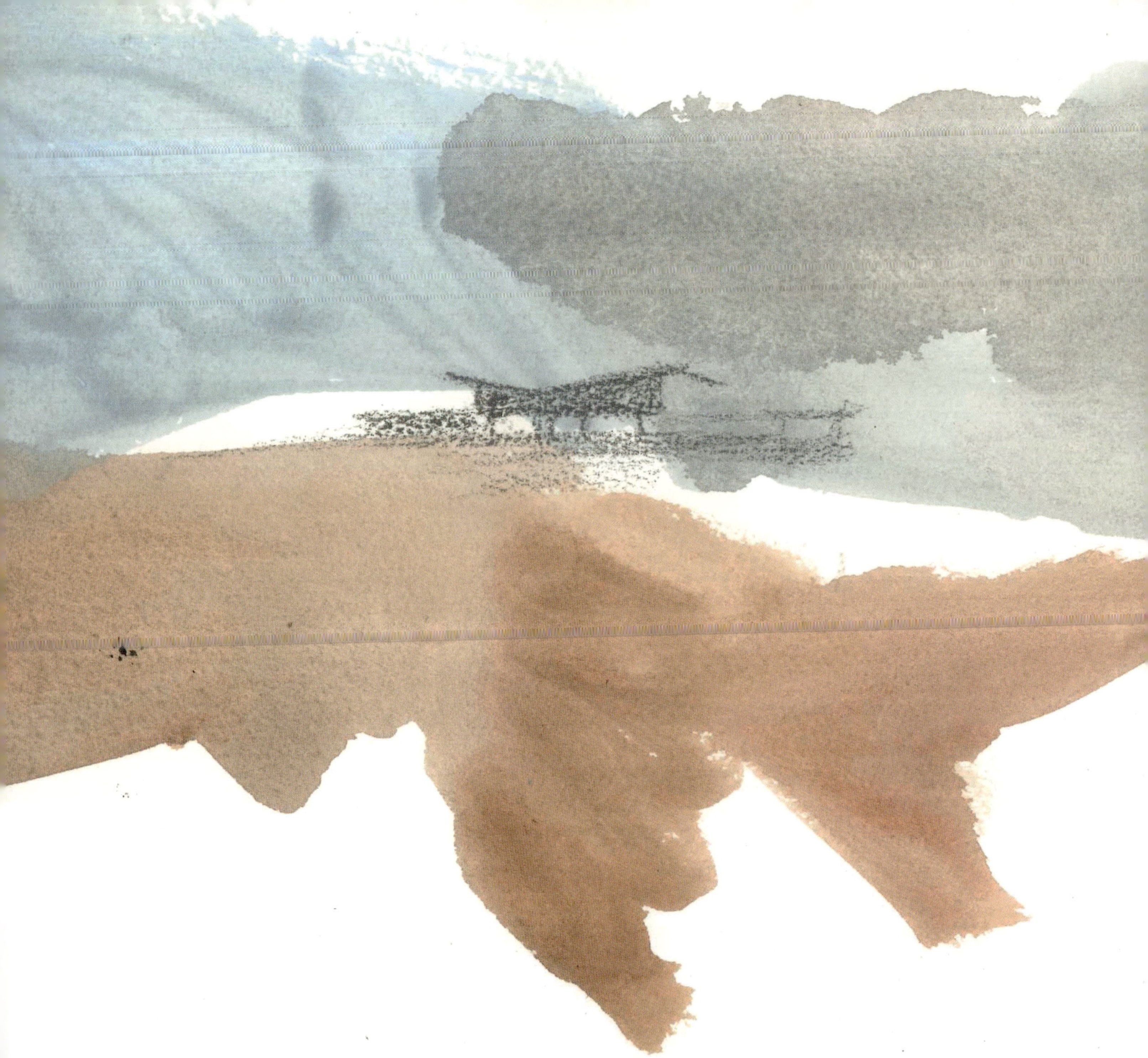

Author's Acknowledgement

Special thanks to my wife for all the support, book development advisor and contributing writer John Warburton, graphic designers Michael Lugmayr and Marcus Hollands at Design by Toko, portrait photographer Jessica Lindsay, Suzie Karkoulas and Lizzie Hayward from my team at Maven, Michael Holt for editorial direction, and, of course, all the architects featured. I would never have gotten this book off the ground without your passionate and invaluable support. I would also like to thank the featured photographers who have kindly provided supporting project imagery.

First published in 2016 by
Maven Publishing, Sydney, Australia
www.mavenpublishing.com.au

Design
Design by Toko

Printing
Opus Group

National Library of Australia Cataloguing-in-Publication entry

Author
Dean Dewhirst

Title
Chasing the Sky:
20 Stories of Women in Architecture

ISPN
978-0-9953825-0-3

First published in the United States in 2017 by Oscar Riera Ojeda Publishers Limited

ISPN
978-1-946226-02-0

International distribution
Oscar Riera Ojeda Publishers Limited
Unit 4-6, 7/F,
Far East Consortium Building,
121 Des Voeux Road Central, Hong Kong
T: + 852-5311-1625

www.oropublishers.com
oscar@oscarrieraojeda.com